# BEHIND THE CURTAIN

## My Life and Rocky Horror

## Martin Fitzgibbon

Grosvenor House
Publishing Limited

This book is published by
Grosvenor House Publishing Ltd
Link House
140 The Broadway, Tolworth, Surrey, KT6 7HT.
www.grosvenorhousepublishing.co.uk

A CIP record for this book
is available from the British Library

ISBN 978-1-80381-652-4
eBook ISBN 978-1-80381-653-1

# Preface

I was on my way to Düsseldorf airport when the train pulled unexpectedly to a halt just outside of Cologne Railway station. The announcement over the speaker system was (of course) in German, a language I wasn't fluent in, but "zehn minuten verspatung" was easy enough. A ten minute delay.

Our carriage had stopped directly opposite The Dome, a large arena that specialises in musicals, and the huge advertising hoarding outside said, in English, "Alive on Stage. The Rocky Horror Show". The Dome seats well over 1,600 people and would sell out nightly for a couple of weeks or more. It was a long way from the 63 seat theatre of Rocky's first home.

My thoughts drifted back to that first rainy night at The Royal Court Theatre in 1973. I was far away, staring out of the train window for a long time...

"Have you ever seen it?" asked the lady opposite. We'd exchanged a few polite words at the start of our journey.

"Yes" I said, "hundreds of times."

"Wow!" she said, in a genuine display of amazement, "then you must really love it."

"I did," I said, as the train started to move on again. "It was a long time ago now."

# CHAPTER 1

Richard Hartley rang me at home one afternoon in April 1973. I'd worked with Richard over three or four years, both live and in the studio. He's a highly talented, composer and musical arranger with a laid-back style of working I much enjoyed. After exchanging the usual pleasantries, he came straight to the point.

"I've got a musical coming up," he said, "at the Royal Court Theatre in Sloane Square, not in the main auditorium, but in a small room upstairs. I need a drummer who can play quietly, and you're the only person I know who can do that."

In case you're wondering, it was intended as a compliment. Having the ability to play quietly was an asset that had served me well, and still does, although, as a kid learning to play, I wasn't sure if my former neighbours would have agreed with that statement.

"Initially, it's for three weeks," Richard continued, "but it's going to transfer for certain. I know you'll love it." He rounded off by saying "it's going to be huge." As a teenager I'd heard the same proclamation, uttered by big men, behind big desks, in big record company offices. Their assurances never materialised and somehow, as I sat listening to their jabbering nonsense, I had an in-built filter that told me they never would.

"Sounds brilliant." I said to Richard. "It's not about God, is it?" *Jesus Christ Superstar* had been successful in the 1970s and was still running in London, and *Godspell* which followed that seemed to be filling any void in the religious musical landscape. I'd played almost every type of gig, some of which I would be happy to forget but had yet to play a musical. I trusted Richard's judgement. If he thought this was something special, it was wise to take note, although to be honest it wouldn't have mattered, I'd have taken the gig anyway just for the experience.

"It's called *The Rocky Horror Show*," Richard said, and went on to outline the plot as best he could. That wasn't easy, but he did enough with references to Charles Atlas, a transvestite Frankenstein figure, and some interesting B movie characters, to convince me this wasn't going to be *The Sound of Music*. It sounded intriguing, fresh, and a lot of fun. After checking the dates to make sure I was available, I was in. I didn't bother too much about the financial rewards, and I'm not sure I even asked.

For the record, it was twenty pounds a week and in 1973 you could get by on that. Nobody enjoyed a lavish lifestyle on that kind of money, but a thousand pounds a year back then was a living wage, and the promise of a transfer to a good size theatre would mean bigger pay days to come. Later on I discovered the cast were only being paid eighteen pounds a week. I imagine the difference was due to the two unions involved, with the Musicians' Union topping Equity, the actors' representatives, by a couple of pounds. With the date safely in the diary, I carried on with my other work and looked forward to what was ahead.

The band's first rehearsal was in a basement studio in London. Richard Hartley was on keyboards. The brilliantly rock n roll Count Ian Blair (think Keith Richards), whom I'd worked with before, was on guitars. Dave Channing, who'd answered an advert in a musical paper for the unlikely combination of a saxophonist doubling bass guitar, was our third band member and with yours truly on drums, we had our four-piece. I managed to double park on the road outside the studio while I transferred my kit down a short, narrow staircase to what had once been the cellar of a Victorian house and now looked like a pretty basic sound-proofed rehearsal room.

After parking the car and setting up, Richard produced sheet music for each of us, with some unusual song titles. This was 1973, a very different era, and the world had yet to experience anything quite like *The Rocky Horror Show*. The song titles came flying out one after the other. "Sweet Transvestite", "Over at the Frankenstein Place", "Science Fiction - Double Feature", "Time Warp", and so on. We had no idea of the melodies or lyrics, but the titles certainly stirred the imagination. I still have some of the drum parts from that day. I rewrote them to reflect the changes that took place over time, so that anyone following me into the drum chair would be up to speed.

The cast had been working on their vocals in a different location, so for now, in order to cue intros into some of the songs, Richard would give us an indication of what was to come. One scene-setting instruction I remember well was for the song "Hot Patootie". Richard said, "Okay, at this point Eddie jumps out of the coke machine." Really, did I hear that correctly? "Then Columbia screams 'Eddie!' and I'll count it in." There was no musical out there to match the genius of that.

On the evening of the second rehearsal, band and cast got together for the first time in the ballroom of a London hotel. It wasn't planned, but after we'd finished our run-through, Richard was on his way there and suggested it would be a good idea if we came too. Count and I readily agreed. Dave had a gig booked and had to pass. I packed up my kit and, after a brief stop at Richard's flat, the three of us moved to another part of town.

It was a warm night and the ballroom windows on the first floor of the hotel were open, giving neighbours opposite the first sights and sounds of *The Rocky Horror Show*. Some stood on their expensive balconies, looking directly across as we worked our way through the show's routines. I wondered what they made of it all. The songs the band played earlier that day now had lyrics and melodies, which made them even more interesting and illuminating. "Sweet Transvestite" was a blast from the off, with Tim Curry (wearing women's shoes to get himself into the role) striding impressively around the room. My first impression of Tim: that guy has a great voice and stage presence aplenty. In a couple of weeks' time, many people would get the full Frank experience and consider my assessment to be understated.

Even from a distance Pat Quinn was gorgeous, with acres of hair tumbling down to her shoulders, and Rayner Bourton (a man with blond hair and a tan) who was playing Rocky clearly agreed, as he seemed to gravitate her way whenever possible. Rayner and I became good friends over the next few weeks. I suspected strongly that his intentions were entirely dishonourable, if perfectly understandable, given the stunning Ms Quinn's assets, and my suspicions were fully confirmed as I got to know him better. Pat was nobody's fool and I'm sure practised enough in male attention to have immediately worked out Mr Bourton's game plan.

Nell was an instant red-haired character, with bags of bravado, masses of energy, and a voice that could easily have stripped the varnish from the wooden panels in that room. She disappeared from the theatre one day during a break in rehearsals, to busk and tap dance down the Kings Road, coming back with a satisfied grin of triumph and a few extra pounds in her spangly show pants' pockets.

Richard O'Brien, with long untamed hair, was already looking the part of Riff Raff and ran around with huge energy on impossibly thin legs. This was his baby, and he was working it hard, as was everyone in the cast. The energy levels were extremely high that day and never abated over the months that followed.

Without exception, all the cast were impressive, but the biggest surprise for me on day one was Jonathan Adams as the narrator. Any fan of *Rocky Horror* the movie will know Jonathan played Dr Everett Scott in the film, but he was never surpassed as narrator. He was totally brilliant in that role and fitted Richard O'Brien's Edgar Lustgarten (British broadcaster and crime writer) figure perfectly. His dance moves in the "Time Warp" were priceless, prompting one newspaper critic to say, "It was like watching a dowager duchess doing a strip." I'm not sure why Jonathan switched roles for the film – his part being taken by Charles Grey as the criminologist – but it's tragic that Jonathan's narrator wasn't committed to celluloid for everyone to share the joy. I'm privileged; I was able to see it multiple times, and I never tired of watching the audience reaction to a masterful performance.

After roughly an hour-and-a-half of rehearsal, I packed my kit and carried it back down the second flight of stairs of the day. I took the sheet music home to give me the opportunity of going through it at my leisure. Rocky's drum score wasn't a drain on my reading capabilities, but when it came to full rehearsals, I wasn't going to be the person who screwed up, and glancing through it at leisure would be useful. From the snippets I'd seen and the songs we'd played together, it was obvious *The Rocky Horror Show* was going to have a massive impact. On the journey home I remembered Richard Hartley's words, "It's going to be huge." I understood why he'd said that and knew he was absolutely right.

The Royal Court Theatre sits at the end of the Kings Road in Chelsea. I'd passed the Royal Court countless times in the past, both on foot and driving. It had a reputation for taking chances, for pushing the boundaries and being experimental in its theatrical productions. It was about to live up to that. As I went through the glass doors of the Royal Court and into the foyer, I was reminded of the Odeon Cinema in Uxbridge – a place I visited as a kid on a Saturday morning matinee. At the box office I explained why I was there and asked where I had to go. A charming lady pointed the way to a staircase behind me, tucked away, almost hidden, in the corner of the room. As I walked up those stairs, the slightly faded grandeur of the foyer gave way to something stripped back and more workmanlike.

# CHAPTER 2

Home was a working-class area of West London, adjacent to Heathrow Airport. Our brand-new council-owned house was built on a piece of land that had previously been a brickyard, with a small front garden and by today's standards a very large garden to the rear. It was plenty big enough to play football and cricket, and I did both constantly. Several FA Cup finals were played out in that garden and in the summer months a five match Test series, with England retaining the Ashes against Australia helped by my heroic efforts with both bat and ball.

A six-foot fence separated our back garden from a disused canal cutting, or "cut" as they were known. The cut had been a way of transporting bricks from the site to the Grand Union Canal a few hundred yards away, and from there to places all over the country. Although the land at the rear of our house was scrubby and contained gravel pits, it had patches of green grass and felt to us as though we were almost in the countryside. From the age of six or so, I could scale the high fence separating us from the cut and go fishing in its murky waters with my brother. We caught roach and dace, watched the (mollies) moor hens, who nested in the bank alongside the voles, and learned to stay clear of the nesting swans whenever they had their young cygnets.

A bad cast from your fishing rod could mean your hook and float getting caught on a couple of old sunken barges in the middle of the cut. A discussion then followed on what we should do, and who should do it. To lose a float by yanking enthusiastically and breaking the line was an expensive option. The alternative solution was for either my brother or me to crawl out on the narrow bits of wooden barge and try to free the line. This called for a bit of plea bargaining. Neither of us could swim, but my brother was quite a bit older than me, and this was usually the determining factor in my favour. The cut probably wasn't that deep, although you couldn't see the bottom and nobody knew what was lurking down there in the thick mud. My parents would have had a nervous breakdown had they known half the stuff that went on in and around that water and the extremely dangerous gravel pits a few hundred yards away, where a local girl from our rival estate had fallen in and drowned.

Horses roamed the wasteland behind our house and would occasionally come to the garden fence for a treat, such as a piece of apple. It was much harder to get close to them any other way. Even when I approached slowly, they would move away, wary of me as if I was going to try and catch them. It would have been impossible for me to reach as high as their nostrils never mind getting a harness over their heads, but it made no difference to their cautionary behaviour.

My other encounter with horses was when Fred, the greengrocer, came to the estate. He had an open wagon with custom-built shelving on each side, which was pulled by a large and very beautiful cart horse. At scheduled times on his round Fred would yell loudly, "Woah!" in a voice that sounded like he gargled with pebbles for breakfast and then smoked a couple of packets of cigarettes for the desert course. His yell was principally to stop the horse but was also a signal to his customers that he was outside in the street and open for business. Fortunately, he always stopped outside our house, and while my mum stocked up on vegetables and fruit, I would go visit the horse. It stood patiently, stock still, and seemed to a small boy like me to be enormous. I always tried to catch the horse's eye behind its blinkers, as if I could in some way silently communicate with this amazingly beautiful animal.

Once Mum had completed her buying, she would allow me to linger for a while whilst our neighbours completed theirs. Then, when he was ready and all business was done, Fred would come alongside the horse at the roadside and, in a much gentler but still throaty voice, say, "Walk on." This was my cue to stand a good way back in case one of those massive hooves came down on my foot. I'd watch and listen to their magical sound as they walked away at a measured pace down the road, until another "Woah" could be heard in the distance.

Slippers lived a couple of doors down from us, and I knew I could rely on him to take care of anything the horse left behind. Slippers wasn't his real name; my brother had nicknamed him that as he always wore white plimsoll tennis shoes. Slippers was a keen gardener, and ghost-like he would silently appear with a bucket and shovel to scoop up any manure left within a hundred yards in either direction of Fred's horse. Then, quickly and just as silently as he arrived, he would slip back down the alleyway to the rear garden, his prize held securely in the bucket. Sometimes he would walk right past me but never say a word. It puzzled me why Mr Slippers didn't speak and felt he had to be so secretive in his actions, but the ways of adults were often beyond my comprehension.

Fred the greengrocer had two horses before he converted to the combustion engine, in the form of an old van. He would stop in the same place outside our house and yell "Woah!" in the way he'd always done to alert every one of his presence, but it was never the same for me. The transition to another kind of horsepower came without warning. I was older now but still too scared and disappointed to ask what had happened to the horses. In my head they retired to a life of contentment and gentle grazing in the countryside somewhere. As long as I didn't ask, then it remained that way. I'm sure Slippers missed them, too, but for a different reason. I guess he moved on to artificial fertilisers for his roses. Such is progress in transportation and horticulture.

We lived on an estate of about 120 houses. Two of my aunties – my dad's sisters – lived on the same estate, and Aunty Dorothy's (Dot) was a place I knew I could always visit and get a warm welcome. Auntie Dot would almost bully me into eating something as soon as I came through the door. She would run through a whole menu of food on offer. Sandwiches of ham, cheese, or both if I chose, chocolate bars, bread and jam, and so on. Her final offering, when I had turned down everything because I'd only come to borrow a cup of sugar or a shilling for the electricity meter, was the fruit course. "Have an apple, banana, orange," she would plead. "You can take one of those;

all of those with you." It's no wonder I was never hungry as a kid.

Because our council estate houses were new, we were deemed "posh" by the older rival estate not far away. A class within a social class, although it wasn't until much later around the age of fifteen that I came to realise how much your place in society, your character, and your prospects for being successful in life could be judged by where you came from rather than who you were. We all lived on council estates. My schoolmates, cousins, grandparents, friends, everyone seemed to be exactly as we were. I had no reason to question the shape or structure of society. It seemed an orderly, simplistic kind of affair.

Dads went out to work, mostly in factories, although some did shifts at Heathrow Airport; mums stayed at home. The bicycle was the favourite and cheapest form of transport. I cycled to school, as did everyone not within walking distance. There were no yummy mummies sat in motor vehicles vying for parking spaces outside of my school gates. I'm not sure we even had school gates. I cycled to my first job on leaving school. A whole mobile army of us on two wheels descended upon the workplace, where there was a bike shed the size of a small football field. Nobody had to padlock their bike. Everyone already owned one, with very little distinction between models or makes. It was a kind of communist, biking society brotherhood, where everyone was equal.

Some mothers did part-time jobs for "pin money". My mum did a couple, but I never questioned why and whether it might have been a financial necessity. I had no reason to suppose that we were poor, although it's possible the reality was very different for my parents. With hindsight, I can see we didn't have much money, but had everything it seemed we needed. Food, heating of a kind in winter, and importantly love.

Both my parents were heavy drinkers. My dad in particular. He'd start early in the morning and drink at every opportunity throughout the day. Apparently, he began drinking as a young boy when my grandmother sent him off to school with a bottle which had a rubber teat on the end. I'm talking about tea. The English obsession with loose leaf tea from the Indian subcontinent that required a strainer to catch the leaves in those happy, pre-teabag days. There was no timetable for a cuppa in our house. It flowed freely and frequently throughout the day; always with a small amount of milk in first, followed by the tea, two large spoonfuls of sugar, and drank as hot as you could stand, as if waiting for it to brew had tested your patience long enough.

Once a year my parents managed to save enough for us to go on holiday, and tea travelled with us. Only very wealthy people flew back then, and although we lived in close proximity to Heathrow Airport and could see hundreds of planes daily, flying anywhere wasn't possible for families like ours. One advantage though, and there were many, to a holiday in Devon or Cornwall was that you could take the Primus stove (a small, portable paraffin-fuelled stove) with you. In the days before service stations or twenty-four hour anything, we would stop enroute and in a layby somewhere, enjoy a brew by the roadside. To avoid the traffic and not wishing to lose any precious holiday time, we always drove overnight. The darkness made the experience of the journey and tea by the roadside even more flavoursome and mysterious for me.

Woolacombe in Devon was a family favourite for many years. Somehow our family had moved upmarket from a caravan holiday, and we'd achieved the social heights of staying in a Guest House, which was one step down the ladder from a hotel, but one up from a Bed and Breakfast establishment. Once the formalities of our arrival at Byways Guest House (which would involve drinking a pot of tea) had been completed, we would hit the beach at the earliest opportunity, the precious portable stove being transported to provide tea throughout the day. Forgetting to take deckchairs or the windbreak with you on holiday would have been inconvenient. Not taking the Primus stove, in its modified old biscuit tin surround to shield the flame, would have been a disaster. Dealing with the stove was my dad's task and one which he relished, as the end result was worth any amount of preparation.

I knew almost nothing about my dad's wartime experiences... he voluntarily joined the Navy, which considering he'd never been outside of the country, couldn't swim, and suffered badly from seasickness, maybe wasn't the best choice. But one of the few things he shared with me was the time he spent in Ceylon (now Sri Lanka), where apparently the tea flowed in Bacchanalian-like quantity and was served free of charge to visiting sailors. For a boy sailor like Dad, it would have been heavenly respite during what must have been a time of unimaginable hell.

I loved our holidays in Devon. The factory shutdown was the last week of July and the first week of August. This was the highlight of my year. I had a home-made chart sellotaped to the side of the kitchen cupboard with a countdown on the number of days before we set off. It started roughly two months out from departure. I'd come home from school and with a pencil cross off the days one by one.

Our preferred beach wasn't the long, sweeping sands of Woolacombe Bay, beautiful though that was, but the smaller, harder to access Coombsgate Beach. When the tide was in, there was no sand, only rock pools to poke around in. It was when the tide retreated and the sand reappeared that my interest was sparked. We would follow the water out, carrying all the beach paraphernalia, find a pristine piece of smooth sand and camp out for the rest of day. The beach was perfect for football and the occasional game of cricket, until the tide turned and the waves began to grow in force. That was our cue for the body boards to come out – a favourite holiday pastime of mine and Dad's. If the surf was good, I'd stay out as long as possible, usually until my fingers started to turn white. When I got back to camp and dried off, shivering with cold behind an inadequately small towel, I was handed a warming mug of sweet tea from the faithful Primus stove.

Back at home, the teapot, kettle, and coal-fed boiler in our small kitchen were all crucial pieces of kit in the Fitzgibbon household. The boiler was the only way of heating our water and it had the added benefit of making the kitchen a warm and welcoming place, especially on cold mornings. The kitchen was the hub of our house – the place where we ate, relaxed, listened to the radio, read, and in bad weather where I played, when being outdoors wasn't a sensible, practicable option. We had no heating at all in the upstairs of our house, and my tiny bedroom frequently had ice on the inside of the windows during winter.

Most mornings, as I remember them, would start the same way. There was no chance of me ever falling out of bed, as the old mattress and underneath it the equally well-worn springs of my tiny second-hand bed, sunk down so low they formed a U shape. I'm not sure if years of sitting behind a drum kit or my first bed are to blame for my round shoulders. It's my excuse anyway. I would literally climb out of that small bed, throwing off the heavy but warming blankets, and scramble as quickly as possible downstairs to the safety and warmth of our kitchen. Dad clocked in at the factory at seven a.m., and by the time I got to the kitchen he had already left for work, which meant the coveted comfortable chair next to the boiler was free and Mum would be too busy to ever be sat in it. Never too busy to make me breakfast of toast and marmalade, washed down with tea, of course.

My older brother Paul was never up before me unless he was going fishing, which wasn't often, so it left the chair free for me to relax into. Unless it was a Saturday morning, when Mr Shard the insurance man came to collect the weekly premium. He would knock and open the back door in one movement and always delighted, for some perverse reason, in putting his cold hands on my now nicely warmed-up neck. I never succeeded in getting out of the chair in time to avoid him, and the simple solution of locking the door never occurred to me. Doors didn't need to be locked back then, and I'm darn sure no door-to-door insurance collectors exist today. Mr Shard was either from the Co-op, or the Pru (Prudential Insurance Company); I can't remember which. My parents had two life policies, and many years later when I cashed them in, they returned around £250 pounds each. A measly sum which wouldn't have scratched the surface of any funeral costs and has confirmed my long-held suspicion of "give us your hard-earned cash now and we'll give you lots more later" being the great scam that it is.

Eventually, when furniture became a more affordable luxury, for some unknown reason we got ourselves a fancy drinks cabinet. If you aspired to appear middle-class back then, and I don't think we did, you might have gone for a portable food warming Hostess Trolley; or perhaps the Goblin Teasmade, which woke you up with an automatically made ersatz form of tea that apparently tasted foul. The idea of an alarm call of tea was appealing, but the apparent quality was never going to be a runner in our house. Our drinks cabinet held mostly mysterious glasses of various sizes, but nothing more than two alcoholic drinks. A bottle of brandy, a spoonful of which would be poured over the Christmas pudding once a year, and a bottle of sherry. My guess is, in the unlikely event of a casual visitor turning down the opening offer of tea and not being tempted by the alternative cup of Nescafé instant coffee (we kept a jar somewhere) suddenly asking, "I don't suppose you have a small glass of brandy, or an Emva Cream Sherry I could have?", my parents could have flung open the doors of the drinks cabinet and provided either in the requisite glass. I don't recall it ever happening, but we were prepared if the call arose.

When I cleared out my parents' bungalow some sixty years later, the cabinet had survived in pristine condition, and those bottles inside were possibly the originals too. I took the alcohol home and with a sense of sadness watched the house clearance boys break up the cabinet, along with other precious "heirlooms" which my parents had struggled to buy and valued throughout their lives but were now deemed worthless and unsaleable. That's life, death, and house clearance, I suppose. In total, my parents' remaining worldly goods earned their estate a measly extra fifty pounds. I was too far away in my head to care about negotiating a higher price.

# CHAPTER 3

I'd made it to the top of the staircase leading to the Theatre Upstairs and was curious to see what lay behind those doors. But there was something else I needed to do beforehand. My car was parked right outside the theatre on double yellow lines and wasn't going to escape notice for too long. I couldn't afford another parking ticket, so quickly transferred all my drum cases to the foot of the foyer stairs and went to find a parking meter. I got lucky a couple of streets away and managed to get back to the theatre within ten minutes or so. The foyer was still empty (perhaps it was a slow day for ticket sales) save for my kit and the box office lady, who nodded and smiled in recognition at my return. It took me three trips to carry everything up the stairs to the top landing and temporarily stack them there. Finally, I had the chance to see what lay behind those black painted doors and where I was going to spend the next few weeks.

Richard Hartley had warned me the room was small, and he wasn't wrong. Several rows of tired looking, red cinema seats sat on either side of a wooden ramp or gangway, which ran down the centre of the auditorium to a tiny stage. Stage left, on a raised platform, was a Coca Cola chest freezer which I knew from our rehearsals was where the character Eddie (Frank's first experiment at making a man), played by Paddy O'Hagan, would appear. Adjacent to the freezer, raised marginally above it, was the "laboratory" where Rocky (Frank's more successful creation), played by Rayner Bourton, would emerge from his bandages for the first time. To the rear of the stage was a white screen, giving the intentional impression that this was a cinema, albeit one which was due for demolition soon. Tarpaulins held in place by bits of scaffolding were draped around the majority of the walls, adding to the illusion that this was a building soon to be reduced to a pile of rubble.

Nine actors, all of whom had song and dance routines, a four-piece band, seats to accommodate sixty-three people, a stage, a ramp, one Coke machine, and a mock-up of a laboratory, all had to fit into this box-like space. It must have taken some head scratching and was close to a work of genius from Brian Thompson, our Australian set designer who managed somehow to squeeze it all in. At the back of the room, stage right, was a miniature lighting desk hidden on a shelf behind a black painted theatre flat, and further still to the rear, a small, elongated dressing room which was to be shared by the whole cast.

Gradually people began to arrive for our first full day of rehearsal. Richard Hartley, whose basement flat was just up the road, was one of the first and showed me where we were to set up. The band area was back behind the "cinema screen", and whilst it was tight back there, I was more than pleased with my lot. I'd had to squeeze into smaller spaces than this one.

Scrim is a material used in the theatre for a reveal effect. Later that week I learned at the end of the show, during the reprise of "Time Warp" the band would be backlit behind the screen or scrim, thus magically revealing us to the audience for the first time. At that point each band member donned a face mask, a top hat sprayed in glitter (I still have mine), and a red usher's jacket. A month into the run I decided I couldn't be seen in detail by the audience and wouldn't bother to wear the face mask that night. After the show Jim Sharman, the director, sought me out to ask why I hadn't worn it. I never heard Jim raise his voice nor lose his temper with anyone, and he didn't that day with me, but I'd been well and truly busted with no excuse to offer. It was a stupid, irrational, and unprofessional thing to do. I apologised and never did it again. From then on, I knew Jim was out there somewhere, still watching and checking every detail, no matter how small.

At Richard's suggestion we set up in a line abreast behind the screen. To my right was Dave Channing on bass guitar and saxophone, then Count on guitars (he played bass when Dave was on sax), and far right Richard on keyboards. The keyboards included the actual Farfisa organ which had been used on the number one Joe Meek song, "Telstar" by the Tornados. As well as giving us an authentic and unique 1950s Farfisa sound, we used it to recreate the effect of thunder during the show. It hadn't been designed to do that, but banging on the reverb unit underneath the body of the organ at the appropriate moment was hugely effective and authentically thunder-like. It worked brilliantly well until giving up halfway through the run at The Classic in protest at its continuous abuse.

Members of the company began slowly drifting in and stopped to say hello to us enroute to the dressing room. Tea arrived, courtesy of nice guy Alkis, one of the assistant stage managers. In this instance Greeks bearing gifts were extremely welcome. After tea and tuning up (yes, we tune drums too), everyone was ready to get our rehearsal underway. The cast appeared from their dressing room, Jim Sharman placed himself on the ramp to give the assembled company a brief word on what we were to do that day, and we were ready and eager to get started.

With the band now in place, we soon launched into our first song. Jim called for "The Time Warp". I shuffled through my sheet music, placed the requisite copy on the music stand, and waited for Count on guitar to kick us off. Drums didn't come in until bar twenty, and that was my first opportunity to judge the volume of my playing against the rest of the band, the cast, and the room itself. The first pass went well. The cast were pleased and at the end of the song applauded us for a job well done. That was a nice touch and made us feel welcome and appreciated. After hours of rehearsing with just a piano it made a big difference to the energy of the song to have the backing of a band.

I made two minor adjustments before we ran the same song again; switching sticks to a lighter pair, and decreasing the amount of dampening on the snare drum to give me a bit more attack. The room wasn't too lively acoustically, and after a few more songs we knew everything was going to be fine. The band weren't drowning out the cast; there was still masses of oomph to give those songs the rock 'n' roll feel Richard Hartley's arrangements had called for; and crucially, given it was his piece, Richard O'Brien seemed pleased as well.

In between the musical action, scenes were refined, ideas explored, and Jim worked his magic, bringing this giant, fun, jigsaw puzzle together. I laughed out loud at some of the dialogue, it was so well observed. Jonathan Adams in his brilliance confirmed my initial impression of him; Paddy O'Hagan, playing Eddie and Dr Scott, was excellent too. Richard O'Brien as Riff Raff, was funny, menacing when required, and the perfect foil to Franknfurter. All the cast were impressive; there wasn't a weak link. However, it was impossible to ignore Tim as the person who was going to be celebrated in his role as the outstanding actor in *The Rocky Horror Show*. It wasn't spoken about at the time, at least not in front of me, but we knew the show overall and Tim in particular was going to have a huge impact when it came to first night and beyond. For the moment, everyone would have to wait a little longer for that to happen.

The day ran smoothly and quickly. We had a couple of breaks which gave me the opportunity to walk back to the car and surreptitiously feed my parking meter. I didn't go back to the Royal Court straight away. Although my head was still full of rehearsals, it was good to grab some fresh air and concentrate on something else for a short while. I wandered further down the Kings Road, a place I was familiar with in my teenage years. Back in the day, it was one of the rare places that sold fashionable clothes, and although I couldn't know it then, some of those shops would rise again selling punk clothing directly inspired by Sue Blane, our costume designer for *The Rocky Horror Show*.

Back at the theatre nearly everyone had returned early and seemed anxious to get on with more work. I checked with Richard Hartley to see if there were any changes he wanted me to make. Happily, he said no, and I took my place back on the drum perch ready for action.

Something else I learned that day was the shadow sex scenes between Frank and Janet, then Frank and Brad, were to take place behind the screen, but a few feet directly in front of me. There was some agile scrambling around by the participants as they jockeyed themselves into coital position, which throughout the run they always managed within the timeframe available. Audiences loved it, especially when Chris Malcolm as Brad discovered Frank was his seducer. It was recently I realised that I'm the only person in the world who can say I watched Tim Curry seduce Janet and Brad every night from a few feet away.

It had been a busy and successful first day, at the end of which Jim announced to the cast their calling time for the morning. And after consultation with Jim, Richard Hartley let us know what time the band would be required. After that, everyone dispersed and disappeared quietly into the night. I have no idea how anyone else felt going home, but I felt good.

# CHAPTER 4

My infant school was a mile and a bit cycle ride from home. There were only a couple of gentle hills to climb on that journey, but it was completely effortless for me, sat in a metal basket behind the saddle of my mum's bike. If it was raining and windy, Mum took the brunt of it, with me sheltering behind her, hands gripping the sides of the basket, my feet on the rests, while she battled her way through the elements.

The infant school stood next to the rectory, which in turn was alongside St Catherine's Catholic Church – a place that my mother, brother, and I attended regularly, but never my dad. He was a good man – in my eyes, a great man – but the only time I saw him in any church was when my brother got married many years later. A hundred yards up the road from the "Infants", as it was known, was the primary school where I was to go in a couple of years or so.

My Godmother, Aunty Mary, was one of the teachers at the infants' school. Eventually I moved into her class under the strict instruction from my mum not to call her Aunty Mary during school time. It had to be the formal Miss Grady to avoid any embarrassment to either of us. Somehow, I understood why this was deemed important and played my role perfectly, as did she, with no sign of preferential treatment towards me.

Infant school passed without any real drama, although one memorable moment came after I'd picked a bulrush from the canalside behind our house and taken it in as an exhibit in a lesson on nature. The teacher (not Aunty Mary) was fulsome in her praise at having this unusual specimen (the bulrush, not me) in our classroom. We'd been asked to come in with a flower or plant of some kind, and the other kids had brought in the predictable run of the mill stuff. My bulrush towered in height and originality over the tiny jam jars of daisies and the odd rose.

Over the weekend I quietly basked in the glory of my teacher's praise and looked forward to going back in on Monday morning to resume my smug superiority. As I walked into the classroom, I could see clouds of seeds floating around the room like suspended snowflakes. The heat over the weekend had released all the seed heads, and the thermal mass in the high Victorian roof was particularly good at keeping most of them up there. The instant the teacher saw me she pointed her finger and yelled abuse at the child responsible for this catastrophic event. My kudos evaporated immediately, replaced by embarrassment and shame. I'm sure I learned something more positive at infant school, but what sticks in my head all these years later is the seeming fickleness of a teacher, the injustice of life through no fault of your own, and how quickly you can go from hero to zero.

Once I'd moved up to primary school and got my first bike, I cycled to and fro in all kinds of weather. I cycled back home for dinner (it was never called lunch in our house) then back to school again for the afternoon lessons. This time there was no-one to shelter behind when it rained or the wind whipped into my face. On cold winter days I'd watch my legs, in the standard issue short trousers of the day, quickly turn from red to blue. Head down, I pushed even harder on the pedals to get to my destination and under shelter as quickly as possible. On two occasions (you'd think I would have learned the first time) I had my football boots wound around the bike's handlebars by the laces, and typically I hadn't planned for one of them getting caught in the front wheel. The hanging boot hit the forks and then the wheel, which stopped the bike dead, sending me somersaulting over the top and onto the tarmac. Apart from the suddenness of the fall and a bit of a shock, I was fine. My main concern was damage of any kind might mean missing football later that day. On both occasions I got up, checked the bike and boots were okay, and with a few scrapes and bruises pedalled on.

Our primary school headmaster was Mr A.B. Hannerfy, whose idea of discipline was rule by fear. It wasn't quite Dickensian, but anyone who thinks it's acceptable to traumatise six- and seven-year-old children belonged in an institution rather than at the pinnacle of the teaching establishment. Even before I knew the meaning of the word, I grew to despise him. Some minor misdemeanour by a pupil resulted more than once in our esteemed headmaster appearing unannounced in the classroom. One I remember vividly was the time he ghosted in and called out a child for the heinous crime of leaving his school mat at sports day instead of returning it to the pile a few metres away. Hannerfy must have seen it. I don't believe any other teacher would have been so petty. In the classroom, a lecture followed from our great leader. This monstrous behaviour would be noted on the pupil's school record. And that school record, he informed us, would follow the hapless child not just to the next educational establishment, but beyond into any future career. Then slowly and dramatically, he withdrew a cane that had been hidden down the trouser leg of his heavy check suit; a trick I was to witness more than once. "This is a lesson to all of you," the crazy sadistic bastard said, and three heavy strikes of the cane on each upraised palm followed.

Luckily my first form teacher at primary school was Paddy O'Sullivan who, unlike his boss, was an innovative and inspiring man, gifted at enthusing the kids in his charge. I wondered what he thought when the headmaster came into his class unannounced. Perhaps he knew in advance, but somehow I doubted that. Although it's not obvious, the well informed amongst you might have guessed that Paddy O'Sullivan was Irish. Ours was a Catholic school with an abundance of Paddy's, a smattering of Shaun's, and a good amount of Mary's in each class.

Mr O'Sullivan taught many subjects, including art, something he was quite brilliant at. Using cardboard boxes and recycled bits and pieces, he built a mock-up of a TV studio, complete with a very convincing looking camera on a tripod and a box-like structure for a TV screen, which was placed on his desk for the news reader/presenter to sit behind. For the bossy types in our class, there was a floor manager whose main role was to count down from five, yell "on air", and point authoritatively in the direction of the "TV screen".

He carried his artistic skills into our history and sports lessons, too. He'd travelled to Pompeii, visited the Colosseum in

Rome, hiked up Mount Vesuvius, and his stories of those adventures were thrilling. To us kids travelling anywhere that involved a boat or a plane was unbelievably exotic. The most we had done was a trip to Southend, or Hayling Island, whereas this man had travelled to parts of the world we read about in books. Pompeii and Herculaneum in particular grabbed my imagination. I loved the idea of the preservation of artefacts, of houses and shops that had been petrified in time. The ruts in the sides of the streets grooved by the wheels of carts were the kind of detail we found captivating.

To fuel this newly discovered passion, our class was divided into Roman legions. I was a member of Hispana (stationed in Britain in the year 43 AD). We had inter-legion quizzes, played inter-legion football matches, and marched to the playing fields a few hundred yards from school, behind our respective banners, made for us by our teacher. The momentum and excitement for Roman Britain grew further when a school trip was organised to the Roman town of Verulamiam, or St Albans in Hertfordshire. The coach trip was a first for me and possibly others too – a real treat for kids who had little chance to go anywhere. The noise inside that coach generated by thirty-five excited kids must have been horrendous.

The amphitheatre at St Albans had been built around the year 140AD and unearthed in 1847. I have a memory of walking around the perimeter, which seemed huge at the time. We weren't allowed to go down to the arena, but anywhere in that place was a thrilling experience and a day out I will always remember. On the way out of the museum next door to the theatre, you could buy broken bits of Roman pottery, which I still have. It was a random jamboree bag, and included in mine was a Roman nail. One of the teachers broke it in half to verify its authenticity, something that still mortifies me. Maybe one day I'll superglue it back together.

There was also music in our classroom, something I enjoyed and was good at. It wasn't on our class timetable, and my guess is our idiotic headmaster was away for the day, so without fear of censure came the opportunity for us all to have some fun. Whatever lesson we thought we were going to have was cancelled.

A case, holding a full-size accordion, was suddenly produced from under Paddy O'Sullivan's desk and the next hour was a magical singalong to all kinds of music. I loved those unexpected moments.

Later, when I moved to secondary school, Mr O'Sullivan moved with us, too. He never taught me again, and in the end I was glad of that. For some reason he'd changed, and not for the better. Maybe teaching older pupils wasn't right for him. Perhaps something was wrong in his private life; I don't know. I knew kids who were in his class and quizzed them about his teaching style, which didn't square at all with how it used to be. I bumped into him a couple of times in the school corridors, and though he must have recognised me, he showed no sign of it. It made me genuinely sad. I wanted to say thank you and let him know how great he had been, but the right moment never came.

Back at St Catherine's Primary School, I moved up from Mr O'Sullivan's class to meet my new form master. I'd had the Irishman, and expected my new master, a Welshman, Mr Jones, would be at least as good. Some things in life disappoint. They say all the Welsh can sing, and when Mr Jones got angry, which he seemed to do frequently, his voice swelled in pitch and volume so by the end of the sentence he was no longer speaking, but singing in a high-pitched, speedy soprano.

"Jonah" had a bad-tempered habit of throwing things at us. His favourite missile was the blackboard rubber. When this was unavailable, having been launched earlier, he resorted to bits of chalk, which carried far less weight and thankfully less accuracy. Eventually, when he'd run out of ammunition, he took to smacking pupils with a school ruler instead. You were called to the front of class, and there the red-faced singing master would wield the ruler from the full extension of his arm, high above his head, to come crashing down onto the palm of his victim's hand. Frequently the rulers broke in half; it happened to me twice. Whoever was in charge of dishing out the rulers in our school must have wondered what the hell was going on.

I wasn't used to this line of teaching. I couldn't recall Mr O'Sullivan disciplining anyone by violence or any other means. This was the same group of kids who had moved en masse to another class, and it seemed unlikely to me that overnight we became an unruly bunch in need of such discipline.

I don't consider what we experienced was child abuse, although by today's standards it might easily be judged as such. It wasn't extreme violence; however, the memory is vivid, and it makes me uncomfortable still.

Another of Jones's eccentricities was refusing requests from anyone who raised a hand to go to the toilet. I think he believed this was some kind of a ploy to get out of class for a few minutes. One day, somebody who'd asked to leave the room and been refused, peed themselves sitting at a desk.

After that, his rule by rulers and throwing practice continued, but at least he cut us some slack whenever someone raised a hand for the toilet.

Messrs Hannerfy and Jones were well matched. To have one psychopath in a school was unfortunate; to be taught by two of them was bad luck in the extreme.

Although he'd been injured by shrapnel in both knees, my dad played semi pro football for Hayes Town after the war, despite (in typical services' black humour) being told by a medical officer that he would never take part in any sport again. I saw him play a number of times for his works team. Even though I was biased, it was obvious he was head, shoulders, and damaged knees above everyone else on the field. With Dad's help, lots of practice from me, and perhaps some inherited natural ability, I got to be pretty good at football.

I captained the school football team, played for a Saturday and Sunday side, and spent most of my out of school hours kicking a ball around with my mates anywhere we could find a grassy space.

The school had arranged for some of us to have trials for the county side of Middlesex. Two dozen or more schools entered their pupils to the district trials, and gradually throughout a long day players were whittled down until eventually the final two sides played off against each other. Fifteen of the remaining twenty-two boys would then be chosen. I played on the left wing, and when they called the players to return in two weeks, the last names on the list were the left-sided trialists. I had to wait until everyone else was called to find out if I was in or not. To make it worse, the official reading out the names did so in a slow, deliberate manner. The very last name, the fifteenth to be read out, was to be the left winger. I knew I'd played well and had overheard my name being spoken about amongst the officials on the touchline, but I was still nervous of the outcome. After an age of waiting, we finally got there. Fourteen names had been called. The last name to be read out was mine. I was now a county footballer and couldn't wait to get home and tell my parents, especially Dad.

A few days later in morning school assembly, Headmaster Hannerfy announced that I was the only boy from our school to have made the county side. He harangued the others for their failure and told them they should look to me as an example of what could be achieved. A small part of the young me grasped the irony of the person who had once severely caned me for playing football in the school playground now indirectly praising me for doing it.

I didn't feel the need to go to grammar school, which was just as well as I failed my eleven plus. I wasn't bothered about passing and hadn't done any revision, but on the day I genuinely tried my best with the paper in front of me. My parents went to a meeting prior to the exam and spoke with Headmaster Hannerfy, who wasn't encouraging about my prospects of passing, nor my future generally. Apparently, he told my mum and dad that he didn't believe I would pass (for once he was correct), and to paraphrase the man slightly, that I "wouldn't amount to very much".

My new school was to be Douay Martyrs in Ickenham, Middlesex – an exciting bus and underground train ride from home. I was fortunate to be attending a brand-new school with excellent, sparklingly clean facilities. We had a gymnasium, tennis courts, metal and wood working shops, a science laboratory, and an arts facility, all of which I loved. I indulged in basketball, rugby, athletics, badminton, and of course, plenty of football. I played football for Middlesex at three different age levels, alongside one other lad from our secondary school, John Morgan, who was an excellent player. Club scouts attended many of those games and there was interest from them in John and me. We spoke about it together and discussed the merits of each club and what we should do. In my judgment, John could have made it as a professional at some level or other, but he chose instead to play rugby. I was now more captivated with music, and have no way of knowing if any alternative route in my life would have been successful or not.

I'd reached the age of fifteen and decision time at school. Should I stay or should I go? I was in the "A" stream throughout secondary school, though never more than an average student. I didn't feel the need to have paper qualifications to secure my musical future, but some of my friends did have ambitions that required exam results. Pete became a teacher, as did Dennis. Others, like my good buddy Glynn, believed in practical skills and that being a hairdresser required nothing more from the English language than he already possessed.

"Have you been on your holidays yet" was the phrase every hairdresser had to learn apparently, along with charming your clients, and having the ability to cut and style hair, of course.

A few years later (at record company expense) I went to a Vidal Sassoon Salon to have my hair cut and tamed. Its coarseness still resembles a Brillo pad at times. On one occasion Vidal himself appeared in the salon, and the great man made his way down the line of chairs, schmoozing the male and female clientele as he went. Finally getting to me, he stopped, fingered my hair, and in a camp voice said, "Hmm, it's just like straw" then moved swiftly on. He didn't even ask if I'd been on my holidays.

Once I had decided to leave school, Headmaster Burke called me in to ask my intention and what plans I had for the future. He was kind enough not to laugh when I told him of my musical ambitions, wished me well, and we parted on the same good terms we'd enjoyed throughout my secondary school years. Word had obviously got around that I was leaving, and next the school priest asked to see me. He was a decent man, who wasn't too priestly or pious for my taste. On this occasion he looked a little world-weary sitting behind the desk, as if he'd had a long day of asking the same question and being told anything but the words he was hoping to hear. What were my plans for the future? he asked.

I rattled on about what I was going to do whilst he sat there patiently. At the end of my excited rambling, he nodded his head slowly, shook my hand, and said, "God bless." It wasn't until later I understood his reason for asking. I thought he was being a good shepherd to his school flock rather than a recruiting officer for the church. Had there been a GCSE in common sense, I would have failed that for sure. I don't think the clergy missed out on me not joining their ranks. The celibacy clause alone was never going to tempt me. Even the promise of free communion wine didn't make up for that.

My dad worked in a local factory. He clocked in around seven a.m. and came home for lunch on his motorbike. If I was around at lunchtime, I would wait for him by the kerbside at the front of our house, knowing that he would give me ride on the bike. We only went a few yards around the small roundabout outside the house, but it was still a treat worth waiting for. I'm sure Dad enjoyed it, too; father and son sharing a few simple, precious moments together. We shared many more over the years; enjoyed each other's company, and were very comfortable in the time we spent together.

Dad enjoyed music a lot and would come to watch me play as often as possible. He'd been an amateur dance band drummer himself after the war, although I never got to see him on stage. An old snare and bass drum lived in the cupboard under the stairs at home, and I would occasionally dig out the snare, bash about on it for a few minutes before putting it away again. Much later, when I got serious about learning, I took drum lessons with my uncle who had also been a dance band drummer. I guess you could say that drumming ran in our family, and if I was to learn any instrument the drums seemed a natural choice.

Uncle Ron, my drum teacher, was my mother's brother and a very fine teacher, too. He gave me good practical advice and solid grounding in technique, taught me a raft of rudiments, and how to read music, which became important for me later down the drumming road. He was the most mild mannered, patient, gentle person anyone could meet. A quietly spoken man who I learned from my mum had won the Military Medal in World War Two for rescuing an injured officer from no man's land. From his demeanour no-one would have guessed.

One of the best moments of my musical life was around five years ago when his lovely daughter Lesley, equally quietly spoken and gentle, came to a concert I was playing. After the gig, Lesley said how much she had enjoyed herself and delivered a killer phrase that still makes me emotional when I think of it. "My dad would have been so proud of you had he been here tonight," she said.

I kissed her on the cheek, gave her a massive hug, managed to whisper, "Thank you, that means so much" and had to walk away.

At fifteen I was living at home, and although musically ambitious I wanted to make some contribution to the household income until "stardom" arrived. My dad had left the factory to become a self-employed driving instructor, and with a business partner had plans to open a petrol station with a car repair workshop at the side. I wasn't at all interested or knowledgeable about the mechanics of cars, but as it was my dad who'd be my boss I figured he would be totally sympathetic to my failings. Luckily for the health of the proposed business, that extremely selfish idea didn't materialise. Planning permission for the garage was refused, and I had to rethink what I hoped was only my temporary working future.

I talked it through with my parents. They were as supportive of my long-term ambition as ever, but I agreed to go as an apprentice in the same factory where my dad had worked for many years. I wasn't sure exactly what this entailed, but I would earn some money and it still left the weekends free for other interests. On day one, I cycled into Drayton Controls, followed my new colleagues through the gates, parked the bike, reported to the office, and clocked in at seven a.m. I learned later that you were given a few minutes' grace beyond seven but would be docked a quarter of an hour's pay if you punched your card at five past the hour.

The factory workshop was large and noisy with the bigger machinery banging away in one corner, and it was here I was going to work. I was introduced to my mentor Nibs, who had worked alongside my dad (I never knew his real name; everyone called him Nibs). He was a decent, patient man and did his best to settle me in. His title was automatic machine setter, a skilled job with four machines under his control. Once Nibs had "set them up", it was my job as apprentice to collect the requisitioned bars of steel from the stores, feed them into the machine, monitor the operation to keep them swarf free, and periodically test the machined parts coming off to ensure they stayed within the correct parameters. Everything was a timed operation and failing to stick to that had to be explained to the shop floor manager Mr Purkis, who occasionally appeared from the office in his white coat, signifying the difference between his status and us brown coats.

It was mostly a male environment, but there were a few middle-aged females who had a bit of a giggle whenever this fifteen-year-old baby-faced apprentice in his new brown coat passed them by. I wasn't fazed or embarrassed by any of their remarks; they only made me smile. One to be avoided though was Cissie Fox, who had a pet monkey she brought into work with her and which sat and shat on her shoulder throughout the day. They say owners and their pets often resemble each other, and although I couldn't possibly comment, there may be an element of truth in that theory. I can't believe anything like that would be allowed today on health, safety, or hygiene grounds. It certainly added character and interest to my new surroundings, and they made a bizarre sight the pair of them wobbling around the workshop. I never trusted that bloody monkey, though, and kept well away from it on every occasion they strayed close.

I hadn't been there more than a week when I was approached by the Union convener who asked if I wanted to join the AEU (the Amalgamated Engineering Union). It wasn't a closed shop and therefore not compulsory to be a member, but it was advisable in his opinion for me to join. I had no idea about what was involved, but was swayed with talk of collective wage bargaining along with other unionised benefits. So, in the spirit of working brotherhood, I said yes, paid my weekly subs, and got my card as a union member. I went to meetings, sat quietly at the back, tried and mostly failed to understand what was being discussed, but enjoyed the cut and thrust of the debates, even though being a union meeting it was fairly one-sided. The most dramatic events took place in the works yard where management and workers' representatives put forward their proposals, standing on top of a wooden packing case. There was passion and loud voices from the Union reps' side and smooth suited, well-groomed reassurance from management.

One of my favourite films is the Boulting Brothers' *I'm Alright, Jack*"; if you haven't seen it, I recommend you do. It paints an amusing if cliched portrait of the British working man, with Peter Sellers playing Fred Kite, a union official who delivers some classic dialogue. Drayton Controls wasn't in any way militant and nor were its workers. It was a bunch of working-class blokes doing their best to get by, do the right thing, and make a living for themselves and their families. Most of those men had served in the Second World War and inevitably that came up in conversation. I assumed that the boastful ones were talking up their role when serving in His Majesty's Forces and those that kept quiet (like my father and my first drum tutor Uncle Ron) had good reason to do so. Even though I was cynical of some, I didn't envy that generation. My life was peachy, and with the 1960s came the birth of much freedom and excitement that they hadn't been able to enjoy. We were emerging from the monochrome existence of the post-war period into one of colour, where everything seemed to come bursting vividly into our lives. Music underwent a revolution, and for a long time Britain showed America what it could do. Clothes and hairstyles became fashionable, colour television arrived in sixty-seven. Motorbikes, cars, and scooters were affordable and gave you mobility; the Contraceptive Pill more peace of mind and freedom to experiment and enjoy. Life, for this teenager anyway, was good.

Al, who played guitar in Crims People, worked in the stores at Drayton Controls, although we rarely got to see each other during work hours. I spent more time in the metals store collecting bars to feed in my machines, and it was there one day that I was involved in a small accident when a heavy bar fell down from high and hit me on the side of the head near my left eye. It didn't hurt at the time and I didn't go down, but I could feel blood running down my face and Jack the storeman said I staggered about on the way to the first aid station. They bandaged me up and sent me to hospital for a few stitches. I still have the scar, although luckily it hasn't destroyed my stunning good looks. It was the storeman's fault for not stacking some new stock properly. I know he was concerned about me but also worried about being in trouble with the management for causing an industrial accident. He didn't need to worry on either count. No serious damage had been done. Then we had George, the self-proclaimed works' war hero who was in charge of setting up four or five machines way over on the other side of the workshop. He was a strange, short, swarthy man with an extremely low tolerance level, who read paperback cowboy fiction and seemingly lived a bit of a fantasy existence. As a new boy I was fair game, and he sidled up to me one day with a tale that sounded as though he and John Wayne had been solely responsible for liberating Normandy in World War Two. Little beady eyes shot over my shoulder as if he expected to be outed by someone any second.

I was polite and tolerant, but he soon gave up trying to impress the underwhelmed me, and I think Nibs had a quiet word in his ear, too. George had a big problem retaining operators for his machines. I couldn't know for sure, but it seemed highly likely they got fed up with his posturing, ridiculous tall tales, and bad temper.

We had a pair of male twins join the workforce who were assigned to work with him, as there were always vacancies on that side of the factory floor. The twins dressed alike, had matching hairstyles, and looked impressively identical in every way. They didn't talk much and didn't mix either, preferring each other's company to any outsiders. Before long George was tearing his Brylcreemed hair out with the pair of them, which amused us as he grumped and groaned his way around the workshop moaning to anyone who didn't first see him coming. The twins went everywhere together, to buy cigarettes (we had a feller called Arnold who sold those and condoms from a locked cabinet by his bench), to the toilets, to eat, and they would always be gone for as long as they could eke it out. A furious George would be out on a search party to all potential hiding places. If they had been sighted, no-one would let on to keep the game going for as long as possible. Then when they finally returned through the workshop – often with George in pursuit – the operators "banged them in" with large lumps of metal being struck against anything that made a decent noise.

When the twins got fed up with the job they'd been assigned, they'd swap with each other to relieve the boredom, even though they hadn't been trained for that specific job. George wouldn't have a clue what was going on until things started to go wrong on both machines. Inevitably, it didn't last. I never knew if they had quit or been fired. Either way, the vacancies on the far side of the workshop returned, which calmed our resident war hero for a while.

I was learning how to make, reshape, and set up some of the tools for our machines, although the majority of my work was ensuring they ran properly and making sure the parts came up to a high standard and passed inspection. When the run was finished, it was my job to strip down the machine and clean it out thoroughly so that Nibs could do his reset for the next job. I was spending a lot of time working in the lubricants used. This was mostly oil, and my arms began to suffer with dermatitis, which was uncomfortable more than unsightly but not something anyone would choose. It was a common ailment amongst some of the workers. I tried elasticated sleeve protectors made of some kind of plastic material, but it didn't help much. It was impossible to keep completely oil free, and protecting my forearms didn't help my upper thighs and legs which were also suffering. The nurse offered sympathy but no practical solution to my problem.

I spoke to Mr Pukiss and said I would have to leave. It meant abandoning my apprenticeship, which wasn't floating my boat while I was intent on a career in music, and me becoming "rash man" didn't make it any more enjoyable. Rather than leave, Mr Purkiss suggested a move to a lighter job, smaller machines as an operator, where I wouldn't come into close contact with anything like the oil I'd been dealing with. He had some vacancies on the other side of the workshop. I felt obliged, as though I had let a number of people down – Dad, Nibs, myself in some ways – so I agreed to the move and ended up working in the elephants' graveyard of the workshop, the place where only the desperate survived. I was now working for George.

It's fair to say that it wasn't a marriage made in heaven. He got under my healing skin from the off, and at one point

I think he got scared that I was going to hit him. I had no intention of doing that, but I wasn't going to take any of his nonsense either. He was definitely wary, his little eyes darting about all over the place as he told me about the unarmed combat skills he'd learnt in the Army. He used the phrase "killer hands", which made me laugh out loud and didn't please him. A few weeks later I handed in my notice, and this time there was no persuading me.

# CHAPTER 5

Most rehearsal days at the Theatre Upstairs began in the same way. The cast were crammed into their tiny dressing room, belting out some classic rock 'n' roll songs, accompanied by Richard O'Brien on acoustic guitar. Ostensibly, this was to warm their vocal cords; an idea which any vocal coach will tell you is a "must" prior to a performance. However, in this case it was as much, if not more, to do with having fun, and fun was something we were all enjoying. If they weren't too busy, my day would begin with either Marion or Alkis, our assistant stage managers, rustling up a drink from somewhere, before I settled in by checking the tuning, and tightening anything on my kit that might have worked its way loose. Gradually the cast, technicians, and musicians would drift into the auditorium until everyone was assembled and we were ready to roll.

Rehearsals were never a chore, and nor at any time did it feel like work as we edged our way towards previews and first night. I'm not entirely sedentary by nature but I do enjoy sitting. Someone once unkindly asked if that's why I decided to play the drums. Well, no, it's just a happy byproduct, and much of this day was spent sitting on the drum stool watching changes to logistics as the cast manoeuvred their way around the set, swopping handheld microphones, dodging the band, each other, props, and future audience members, who would be so close as to be almost on stage with them.

By now everyone had learned their lines perfectly. I can't recall any cast member drying, stumbling their way through the dialogue, or at any point forgetting a lyric. The theatrical expression is being "off the book", which was just as well; if you faltered, there would be no prompt on this show to help you out. I can't recall the band messing up either, although we had little to no excuse with our musical charts to guide us.

I didn't need those parts any more and had committed the songs to memory, but nonetheless they were a reassuring presence, and I would glance at them prior to each song, just in case. Richard Hartley would conduct us into the beginning of each song with over-exaggerated, silent gestures. As we sat at different ends of the line, he would stand so I could see him start the count in, then quickly dart back down again so not to miss his first note on the keyboard.

The only hitch I can remember in the latter stages of rehearsals was Tim wrestling with the surgical gloves he had to put on. During the performance they would often fail, despite the best efforts of the crew who applied copious amounts of talcum powder to the insides. When the gloves split or became uncooperative in some way, Tim carried it off brilliantly, as if it was part of the script. I always thought it funnier in than out, and Jim liked it that way, too. It felt to me like we were ready, even before we were due to be ready. There was a buzz about the place, a feeling of expectation and excitement, and this grew in intensity once dress rehearsals began. With the cast now in full makeup and costume, it kicked the performance level up another notch and helped in the realisation of their characters. By now I had a complete picture of how the show would work. Scenes we had rehearsed out of sequence fitted together in chronological order. It felt perfect to me. The time had come to see what the outside world made of it all.

Saturday, 16th June, 1973

The first preview.

I learned that previews are a kind of dress rehearsal with a tame audience. A chance to have a run through amongst "friends" and, if necessary, make changes before the newspaper critics view the show on opening night. For me, knowing no better, a preview was as good as a first night; a chance to play in front of a live audience, and something I was looking forward to immensely.

There was a production playing downstairs at The Royal Court – *The Sea*, starring Coral Browne, wife of horror movie actor Vincent Price. In order not to disturb anyone with our music, Rocky was to start at 10.30pm Monday to Friday, and on a Saturday we wouldn't begin until 11pm, which was better still. Inadvertently, late performances gave us an extra edge and exactly the kind of atmosphere we were looking for. Rock 'n' Roll and Rocky belonged to the night.

Those in house for our first preview were mostly friends of the cast, theatre staff, and so on, but friends or not they loved it. They whooped and hollered in a genuine display of pure pleasure. It wasn't a bunch of friends trying to make their mates feel good; it was an exhilarated group of people who felt life was slightly more interesting than it had been an hour-and-a-half earlier. To my eyes and ears, it ran perfectly, although I was sure Jim would find something he wanted to work on. Afterwards, Richard Hartley disappeared for a swift consultation and on his return reassured us there were no issues for the band. He thanked us and we were told what time to be in on Monday. It had been a brilliant start, as we knew it would be. The next day was Sunday and a day off. I didn't really need a day off. I wanted to get back and watch a new group of people being blown away by this extraordinary show.

Monday, June 18th, 1973

I arrived early as usual, but rather than disturb Jim and the cast who were running through something, I went back downstairs and into the pub next door for a while until the band were required. Eventually we were called and Jim decided to run the "Time Warp" curtain call with the full band. After two passes, he was satisfied. We were done with time to kill, and with some of the stage crew, I adjourned to an eating house down the Kings Road to grab a bite to eat.

I remember less about the second preview with the exception of the audience reaction. It was the same enthusiastic joy and surprise which I was already coming to expect, and we hadn't officially opened yet.

Tuesday, June 19th, 1973

First night:

"We regret that latecomers cannot be admitted under any circumstances," said the printed programme. It also mentioned there was no smoking allowed in the auditorium and that the show would run for ninety minutes with no interval. If you were a smoker, enjoyed a drink, or suffered from incontinence, then it could have been an uncomfortable hour-and-a-half ahead.

It's been well documented that it rained heavily that night, and I can confirm that's true. I made a dash to the foyer and up the now familiar three flights of stairs, where there was an excited buzz about the place. It didn't take many visitors to fill an already overcrowded dressing room, so I left early, and as I was coming out, the lovely and hugely talented Julie Covington was on her way back in. We wished each other good luck in the traditional theatrical "break a leg" fashion, and I made my way back behind the screen. Sitting on top of my snare drum were two first night cards. One from Richard O'Brien and the other from Tim; I still have both. It was a nice touch which meant a lot and typified the inclusive nature of this show. As you would expect, neither has flowers or a sentimental rhyming verse. Tim's is in postcard form, has a picture of a sword swallower with a caption about bad habits; and the one from Ritz is a black-edged funeral card which says "With Heartfelt Sympathy and Condolence". I would have expected nothing less.

The band had to be in place well before the audience were allowed in, to hide our presence behind the screen. We were a secret to be unveiled, as was Pat Quinn, preparing to sit silently on a small stage covered by a piece of gauze within a few feet of the audience. She had done this at both previews and I'm not sure how Pat managed it. There was no movement from her at all and it seemed she was hardly breathing under there. As people filed past to take their seats, I'm sure some were convinced it was a mannequin on stage and not a real person. Another myth that has passed into Rocky folklore, is that some audience members physically prodded Pat to see if she was real. I assure you it never happened. The band had the best seats in the house, and behind the screen we could see everyone in the audience as well as all the action in the auditorium.

I've also read that the King of Hammer Horror movies Vincent Price was there on first night with his wife Coral Browne. I see why it's plausible, as Ms Browne was appearing in a play downstairs. It's a good story, but also not true. Mr Price is a distinctive looking gentleman and Ms Browne a striking woman; both would have been impossible for me to miss. I looked really closely that night and recognised no-one in the audience (that was to change within days), although I was told the biggest theatre critics in the country were out there. They were all unknown faces to me.

I wondered if the ushers knew who the newspaper critics were, and if so, would they go easy on them so not to undermine the chance of a good review. If they did, it wasn't obvious. There was no discrimination, and with only sixty-three people to harass, their masked, silent menace was spread evenly around the room. The ushers' repertoire broadened over the coming weeks as their confidence and imagination soared, but straight out of the box Paddy O'Hagan was beyond excellent. His slightly menacing, hunched figure and insistent beckoning with witchy fingers entertained everyone, apart from his victims.

I guess those critics had seen most things in their long careers; I'm not sure if they had witnessed a more interesting opening to a show than this. It was Jim Sharman's reputation as a director that had drawn those big names here, and if they thought this unusual, they were about to be taken on an even more memorable journey.

On an unseen signal, the ushers made their way towards Pat and spoke for the first time: "Glad you could come tonight." The unveiling revealed our usherette, complete with her Strawberry Time ice cream tray; Richard Hartley counted the band in, and we were officially underway with "Science Fiction Double Feature" – the first bars of a show that would reverberate around the world for decades to come. Pat charmed the pants off everyone that and every night with her performance as the usherette. Only those who saw it will know how adorable and locked into that character she was. *Rocky Horror* film-goers sadly lost out on that experience, but at least her vocal performance is recorded for posterity on the Original London Cast recording. Of course, Pat was equally compelling in her role as Magenta. It's a tribute to her acting ability that she was able to pull off two very contrasting roles with the same conviction and brilliance.

Jonathan Adams had quietly slipped in through the main doors and mingled with the audience pre-show before taking up his reserved seat on the front row, stage right. In a show of many surprises, he was another when he stepped on stage with his book and announced, "I would like, if I may, to take you on a strange journey."

Every high point – and there were many in this show – the cast hit with precision, and it's unfair of me to single out one performance above all others. However, Tim's entrance was, as you would expect, a triumph. It's impossible to describe the impact it made, and that night I watched the faces of the critics to try and gauge their reaction. I had no idea what they might be writing later, but if the copy they posted mirrored their demeanour, I knew we would be fine.

After the curtain call and the final notes of "Time Warp" died away, the band had to sit and wait for the audience to clear before we were "released". By the time we were free to join the excited throng in the dressing room, it was even more crowded back there than usual. I left it to Richard Hartley and Count to be our twin representatives and looked forward to the catching up with everyone at the First Night celebratory party.

It was a short journey by car down the Kings Road to The Furniture Cave at World's End – the venue for our celebration. The Furniture Cave rather grandly described itself as an Antiques Emporium and was an unusual but inspired choice by our impresario Michael White. It was by invitation only and happily my name was on the list, which got me past security at the gate and into an open courtyard. There were plenty of people already there, none of whom I knew, so a drink seemed to be a good place to start. Gradually the cast began to arrive, all in great form of course. There was some soothing taped music and a stripper, who was the only booked entertainment for the evening. She performed out in the courtyard and had a signature move that's difficult to explain politely but made Tim and myself laugh out loud as we watched.

I stayed for a couple of hours or so, long enough to congratulate all those who weren't hidden too deeply in a scrum of admirers before I headed off. The critics had filed their copy, and in a few hours we would know the verdict. It had stopped raining long ago; the morning air was fresh as I walked back to the car and drove away towards the Fulham Road. It had been an unforgettable night.

# CHAPTER 6

When I arrived at the theatre, everyone appeared to be in a good state, with no ill effects from lack of sleep or excess amounts of alcohol. Spirits of a different kind were high, and rightly so. The critics' reviews were in, and they were much as everyone expected but nobody had wanted to say out loud. They made incredible reading, and as a result *The Rocky Horror Show* had become... literally... an overnight sensation. Enquiries for tickets at the box office had the phone ringing off the hook.

Jim Sharman seemed happy with the performance (I don't recall him wanting to change anything). Richard Hartley was content, too, and already asking if I would continue beyond our scheduled period of three weeks. We were only day two into the run, and it seems talks had been on going between the Royal Court and Michael White about extending the tenure of the Theatre Upstairs. There was a limit on the number of weeks we could carry over. Two, to be precise, as there was another production following on from ours.

Our producer Michael White didn't have a huge amount of time to source another venue for *Rocky*. Michael had a hit show on his hands and was keen to maintain the momentum by transferring to another home as quickly as possible. With fantastic reviews and word of mouth publicity, all you needed was a building to house this production and ticket sales were guaranteed. I've read more than once about why we ended up in the Classic Cinema in the Kings Road – *Rocky*'s second home. The popular, oft repeated version is the decision makers didn't want to transfer to a well-established, slightly stuffy, West End theatre, preferring instead the tackiness and authenticity of a falling down, soon-to-be-demolished old cinema. It's true that a decrepit cinema is the setting for *The Rocky Horror Show*. On the surface, to house it in the Classic would seem the perfect marriage. To add to the urgency, Michael had the perfect cast who were all available, with the exception of Julie Covington.

My take has always been this. As far as I'm aware there was no "dark" West End Theatre, and it could be months before that might be the case. Even then it would require fitting out, causing further delays and zero income for our impresario if he wanted to retain those cast members on exclusive contracts. The Classic was available and wouldn't cost Michael much to build a set; it was already down-at-heel and due to be demolished in a few months' time. The developers had nothing to lose and struck a deal that suited both parties.

Selling two hundred and seventy or so tickets at the Classic would prove to be easy. Getting hold of one of sixty-three at the Upstairs was a massive problem, which even I struggled with. Luckily, Richard O'Brien was about to send two back to the box office and I was in the right place to intercept them. After a couple of hasty phone calls, I arranged for my dad to pick up my girlfriend en route and get to the theatre in double quick time.

Given the sexual content, I wasn't sure if sitting my girlfriend and my dad together was a great idea. However, he was always curious (in a musical sense) to see and hear what I was doing, and this was likely to be the only opportunity to see the show in its original home. I left the tickets at the box office for collection, and from my quiet seat behind the scrim watched them both come in, hoping they wouldn't be "ushered" too badly. It made me smile to see my dad sat out there amongst the hip crowd of the day. I remember us going to buy my first drum kit at Jim Marshall's music shop in Ealing West London. Dad had funded and ferried me around everywhere and never once complained about anything, nor lost his enthusiasm or support for what I was doing. I tried to repay that love and his love of music wherever and whenever I could. So, it was entirely fitting that he was there on this leg of the journey and had more than earned his place.

We met up after the show, which he enjoyed immensely. He was holding a Time Warp instruction leaflet thrown into the auditorium by Richard O'Brien during the reprise, along with a show programme. My girlfriend told me later that there had been the odd uncomfortable moment during the shadow scenes, some buttock shifting on one of those battered old cinema seats, but it seemed we got away with it.

Being the hottest ticket in town meant a lot of celebrity faces just about every night. I've never been starstruck, but it was interesting to see those celebs off duty in their civvies, and as I've said, being able to watch the audience and the action at the same time was a unique position which I don't believe has been replicated in any production since.

This sudden popularity meant some invention was required when you didn't have a ticket and were desperate to get in. Some pleaded at the box office, others tried blagging their way in, including one guy who claimed to be me. It was a surprise when Chris Peachment, the stage manager, came upstairs to check that I was "there". Chris said, "I've got this feller downstairs who says, 'You've got to let me in. I'm the drummer.'" Maybe he'd heard it was the best seat in the house.

On our second night, June 20th, record producer Jonathan King was hanging around in the auditorium after the show. As I walked past, I heard him say to his mate, "They take their time coming out" in a mildly irritated, impatient way. I assumed he was waiting for someone, probably Richard O'Brien, to come out front to meet him. The pair were eventually taken to the dressing room, and it was there, on the strength of seeing *Rocky* for the first time that JK proposed making a cast album, something which happened a few weeks later. I got to see him quite often after that, including making the album, of course, but I never truly discovered whether he had any musical ability or not. I might question Jonathan's credentials as a record producer, but as a businessman with a nose for an opportunity, he was right in the moment and shrewd enough to invest in *Rocky* from the beginning.

There was one person not free to sign on for the extra two weeks at the Upstairs – Dave Channing, our bass player. Dave had another gig booked in his diary and he gallantly wanted to honour his commitment. I spoke to Richard Hartley about a possible replacement, someone I'd worked with a good few times – Dennis Cowan. Dennis was a former member of the wonderfully eccentric

Bonzo Dog Band, who had a couple of hit records, including "Urban Spaceman". As far as I'm aware Dennis is the only male to appear on "Top of the Pops" (a long running BBC TV music show) minus his trousers. I haven't checked, but I'm sure it's out there somewhere on YouTube. The Bonzos, led by the charismatic Viv Stanshall, would suggest Dennis wear something (or in the case of his trousers, not wear something) on TV shows, and being a good-natured guy Dennis would go along with it.

We had a band rehearsal where Richard checked him out, and Dennis was on board for the final two weeks of the run and beyond. He did a brilliant job, slotting in perfectly as a person and player.

The roof leaked at the Theatre Upstairs, and neither was it secure enough to stop a thief breaking in one night and disappearing with Dennis's beloved Fender Bass guitar. Nothing else seemed to have been taken, but it was disturbing and upsetting. Selfishly, I was worried in case something of mine went missing too, so Dennis and I went to see the lovely Harriet Cruikshank, manager of the Upstairs. She was hugely sympathetic, but not able to reassure us that this was a one-off. Harriet explained that the theatre had a night watchman responsible for security. "But," she said, "he sleeps." I thought I'd heard incorrectly, but Harriet went on, "We know he's not supposed to, but he sleeps." That sounded to me like a cracking gig, so I flippantly asked if I could have his job.

"It would save me having to go home, and I could use the extra money," I said.

Dennis wasn't amused by my attempt at humour. He'd lost a precious guitar that had been his for decades.

By a bizarre coincidence, Dennis's girlfriend was travelling on the London Underground that day and, unaware of what had happened, sat opposite a young guy with a very familiar guitar case. She kept looking at it, knowing it belonged to Dennis, but she was too frightened to challenge the young male. Pre mobile phones, there was no way of checking what had happened. A few stops later, the young guy got off, carrying the never-to-be-seen-again guitar in its case.

July 20th

Our Theatre Upstairs experience had been amazing. It's difficult to put into words how the cast wowed the audience each night, and the show that came at you from every angle continued to delight and surprise everyone. It was packed every night, which wasn't hard with only sixty-three seats to sell, but being the hottest show in town those seats could have been sold many times over. It had been a pleasure, but after six weeks at the Theatre Upstairs, it was time for us to go. There was one final show to play in this never-to-be-forgotten place. Our last night... or so we all thought.

I arrived around 10:15 for the eleven o'clock show and was walking through an empty foyer when coming towards me was our guitarist Count, with his arm around the shoulder of Mick Jagger. If you screwed your eyes up a bit, you might have thought it was Mick and Keith, as Count was almost a doppelgänger of Mr Richards. I'm pretty sure Count had never met Mick; however, he was never shy in coming forward, which was part of his undoubted charm. Trailing behind the pair, dressed immaculately in a white trouser suit, looking somewhat left out and slightly fed up, was Mick's wife Bianca. All three passed without even a glance my way from Count, who was deep in conversation, breathing into Mr Jagger's right ear. Pat Quinn was also in the foyer and had been similarly ignored – or in Pat's case, she believed totally snubbed. Pat said to me, "The bastard. Count goes out of his way to say hello to me every night and then totally ignores me when he's with Jagger."

Mick and Bianca had gone upstairs, mistakenly believing the show was to start at 10:30 instead of eleven, only to be sent back down again. I guess it wasn't often that Mick was refused entry somewhere. I carried on up the stairs and it was obvious something odd was happening. There was a commotion going on at the back of the theatre with a crowd of people hanging around the dressing room area.

There was an awful lot of glitter used during the show. It was thrown around liberally amongst everyone, even some of the audience got inadvertently involved because they were so close to the action. But no-one had ever complained; it was part of the fun. Glitter back then was made of glass and somehow Rocky Rayner had accidentally (I assume, but you never know) got some glitter down his briefs. This had then gone underneath his foreskin, causing cuts in the head of his penis, which had in turn become infected in some way. Rayner was in agony, while a curious bunch of less than sympathetic people were queueing trying to get a glimpse of the problem penis. Eventually a doctor advised Rayner that he couldn't go on that night and the show would have to be cancelled.

Harriet Cruickshank took it upon herself to inform the Jaggers that the show had been cancelled because "Rocky's got a problem with his cock". Mr Jagger allegedly replied, "Haven't we all!" It's such a great comment, I really hope it's true.

Mick did eventually get to see the show at the Classic. We were told he was coming, and this time he arrived like a true superstar, last minute, just before "curtain up". Waiting outside the theatre to greet him was his newest best buddy Count. I never asked what it was they had discussed, nor if Mick had enquired about the health of Rocky's cock.

# CHAPTER 7

Eventually Bobby Ward grew to be well over six feet tall, but it took him a while to get there. We were fifteen when we first met, and he could easily have passed for being twelve years old. He was a skinny kid, five feet nothing tall, with shoulder-length hair, bags of energy, the right amount of attitude, and a fantastic singing voice.

I heard about Bob and his band The Outer Limits when they won a national music competition. The local newspaper was fulsome in its praise for everyone but mentioned the band's lead singer in particular as the prime reason for their success.

I needed to check this out and went to see Bobby and his band play at a local outdoor event. They weren't halfway through the first song before I'd decided I should definitely be working with this feller and conceitedly that I was a better drummer than the one they had that night. On stage was this diminutive figure with a huge voice and bags of confidence. He was captivating, brilliant, and the focus of everyone's attention, including mine.

A short while later, the competition winning band broke up (as bands tend to do) and Bob was looking for a fresh bunch of people to work with.

Somehow, he'd heard about me, and I was asked to audition. I had to compete with two other drummers, and after busking my way through a half dozen songs was asked if I would like to join. It was an exciting time, my first proper band, and with Bobby out front I knew we would definitely garner a lot of attention.

We worked up an approximation of some Soul and Motown songs wherever we could find a free rehearsal place. A farmer's draughty old barn in exchange for guitar lessons; a boys' approved school (there was almost a riot when two of our girlfriends came along); and most bizarrely of all a local slaughterhouse. The odd sheep's head hung from the walls along with dubious bits of animals' intestines in sacks on the floor. There was no heating in there and the giant cold rooms didn't help generate any during the winter months, but we considered ourselves lucky to find a place that would allow us to rehearse for free.

Despite our awful band name – Crims People – which was a play on the word criminal (we knew a few), the band progressed quickly from local gigs onto the London music scene.

Al and Tony were older and able to drive, so with a loan we got a van, and after a rough house pub gig in the East End of London, we also acquired a manager.

A middle-aged guy with glasses came over and introduced himself as Andre, told us he was in music management and without question he could get a fabulous band like us a record deal and lots of prestigious work. Andre drove a beautiful Rolls Royce car, which was the ultimate symbol of success back then and certainly gained him a huge amount of kudos with us. He wore a smart suit and had printed business cards, which, to our naive eyes, gave him even more gravitas and importance.

Discussions began on Andre signing us. To help facilitate that, he drove down for a band meeting at my parents' house. The Rolls was parked right outside, which stunned everyone in the neighbourhood. Kids came out to stare at something they had never seen before, whilst curtains twitched as their parents opted for a more secretive viewing.

We cruised around London in the "Roller" feeling like the superstars we were definitely not but aspired to be, and then rolled on up to see the movers and record company shakers who could make those dreams a reality. I've always been fairly well grounded, but I admit there was something about getting out of a Rolls Royce in the busy London streets and briefly being the centre of attention that gave me a smile and a bit of a swagger.

To add to his impressive lifestyle, Andre had a large basement flat in Kensington – another indicator to us of his obviously successful musical management ability. He ferried us around to a few of the biggest music venues of the day, like the Marquee in Wardour Street Soho, run by John Gee, a friend of Andre's, and we were made to feel important when they waved us through as guests. We played some of those clubs, too, like the "100 Club" and "Tiles", where we supported The Merseys, and their drummer stole a pair of my drumsticks. I hope to find him one day. Some things you never forget!

It was later we discovered Andre was Andy, a chauffeur – hence the car and the smart suit. His rented Kensington flat was affordable by subletting most of the rooms, one of which wasn't a room at all, but a cupboard under the stairs just big enough to contain a small single bed and inhabited by his "nephew" Billy, who we never met as he always refused to come out of the cupboard. In fairness Andy had some great contacts, made us laugh, got us gigs and into places that otherwise would have been impossible.

The gigs got bigger and better, not because we were a great band – far from it – but we rode along comfortably on Bob's coat tails. It didn't take long for me to realise that mixing it with some of the big-name bands of the day was a whole different ball game, and instrumentally we weren't anywhere near close enough. All the record company interest we were getting was for one reason and it wasn't the musicianship. Deep down the other guys must have known it too, but they were clinging onto what they perceived to be their one big chance of success.

Mick, a fine rhythm guitarist who held a lot of our songs together, refused to sign a contract and decided he wanted out to spend more time with his new girlfriend, rather than bumming around with us. Now a four piece and no better for it, we made our first recording at Regent Sound Studios in Denmark Street, London's Tin Pan Alley, where the Rolling Stones had made their debut album. It was a big, important day for me, and I didn't sleep much the night before. I was finally going to experience what making records was all about.

My lasting memory of that day was from the drum booth, watching the engineer with his feet up on the mixing desk reading a newspaper throughout the whole of the session. He put down the *Daily Mirror* briefly when we listened back to our efforts in the control room, only to make no comment and pick the paper up again as soon as we went back out for another take. It was far away from how I hoped and expected the creative music-making process to be.

The session at Regent Sound had been booked and paid for by a record company, and the results went back to the company chiefs before being relayed to us. It wasn't encouraging. Luckily, I came out of it as doing a good job, especially at sixteen years of age. Bob got top marks, of course, but the other two guys were brutalised.

We did an audition for Pye Records in their number two studio, with the odd choice of Cyril Stapleton in charge of the session. Mr Stapleton was a violinist and band leader of my father's generation. I took my dad along – or rather he drove me – as he had an interest in meeting Mr Stapleton, a famous figure in the world of dance and jazz bands just after the war. Had we been the greatest rock band in the world I doubt Cyril would have been the man to realise it. He was perfectly pleasant, quiet, a bit reserved perhaps, and said nothing very much. I knew what we'd recorded wasn't going to go anywhere. It wasn't good enough, but I was getting more recording experience and more confident with each visit to the studio. Plus, on this occasion it made my dad happy, which made me happy, too.

A couple of smaller labels showed enough interest to put us through our studio paces. At all of them nothing improved. The recordings we made only emphasised the weaknesses in the playing and reinforced my feeling that the inevitable break-up was around the corner. Tensions began to rise as Al and Tony could see their frailties being exposed, and the constant negative feedback was hard for them to take. It became a very unhappy time. Despite fall-outs and ongoing discussions, we had dates to fulfil and carried on playing those in and around London.

Bob and I saw a band called The Move on TV one night, and at the beginning of their song Night of Fear", a dwarf came bursting out of the bass drum. This slightly bizarre piece of theatre appealed to us. Bob looked at me and grinned. "I could do that," he said.

*Why not?* We thought. So, around at my parents' house we tried Bobby and my bass drum out for size. It was hilarious as Bob curled himself in a ball and squeezed his way into this awkward, round space. He made it into the twenty-two-inch kick drum without too much difficulty, but then had to sort of roll out again. Still, it had worked in a fashion, and we figured if it made us laugh then it would have the same effect on other people. Next, we doctored the kick drum's front head and slid the hoop over the drum. As long as Bobby kept still (there was no room for him to go anywhere, after all), it stayed in place. More hysteria followed as I asked if he was alright hidden in the drum. This muffled, scrunched-up sounding little voice replied that he was fine, and then we were both helpless with laughter again.

We explained our plan to the other guys, who thought it totally unnecessary, as in their view we were knocking audiences over already. But Bobby had the majority say on what should happen, and with me adding my support to the idea, we won the day. It was agreed we would try it at the next suitable gig. This would only succeed if there were stage curtains so we could quickly set up unseen and install Bob literally seconds before we went on. The first time we tried, it worked. The band went around the song's intro a couple of times, then over the mic Al went into the big build-up, introducing our lead singer, the phenomenal Bobby Ward. Tony and Al turned and looked to side stage. So did the audience, in expectation of someone appearing from the wings. Rolling out of the drum came Bob. This surprise floored the audience, and coupled with his big voice in that tiny frame, it stunned the punters. After the gig they lined up to tell us how brilliant this, and we, had been. The second time we tried was better still, with another great response from everyone, including the other bands on the same bill. We were on a roll... or at least Bobby was.

The pirate radio stations of the 1960s, Radios London and Caroline, were circumnavigating the broadcasting rules of the day by anchoring just outside the UK's maritime limit. Pirate radio was a massive shot under the waterline for the BBC, who hadn't catered for teenage musical tastes at all. There was nothing sexy about the British Broadcasting Corporation. It was this crusty institution where broadcasters wore a suit on radio even though they couldn't be seen and had plummy upper-class accents which didn't resonate with the mass teenage population. Just by listening to the pirate stations we felt we were complicit in something a bit naughty, something on the edge of legality, which made it glamorous and anti-establishment at the same time.

Radio Caroline and London started sending over their DJs to gigs on the mainland, and we began playing a lot of those shows. The band got plugged on the pirate stations for days preceding the event, which was fantastic publicity despite being called "Crimes People" most of the time.

We did a big show with Ed Stewart, and the other DJ that night may have been Dave Cash; I can't be completely sure. Both eventually went on to work for Radio One, the BBC's totally inferior attempt to cater for soap dodging teenagers.

At the Radio Caroline gig we were one of three bands playing on two stages. The first band played, and curtains were pulled across on the other stage allowing us to get set up. It was an ideal opportunity to employ the kick drum trick, and we thought it might give us further kudos with the pirate radio boys.

We were the second band on and got prepared, with Bob squeezing into the drum at the very last minute. Mr Pirate DJ made his big introduction. The band struck up, curtains went back, and as before, we started going around the intro a couple of times. Al strode to the mic with the hint of a swagger and delivered Bob's cue. I turned my head to look side stage as before. From the corner of my left eye, I was waiting to see the rabbit roll out of the hat, but all I could see was the kick drum rocking around, more than it had done before. The rocking became more pronounced. The drumhead came off, but no Bob appeared. From the front it must have looked as though a child was having some kind of seizure in there. A poor distraught kid had been cruelly stuffed into the band's bass drum and looked to be in need of urgent medical attention.

I kept playing, but the drum was now moving away from me like an out of control washing machine on a spin cycle. I had to stretch my leg further and further forward to keep my foot on the kick drum pedal.

All bass drums have a spur on each side to anchor the drum in place. The spurs have a sharp point on one end that digs into the floor to stop the drum creeping forward. Today they're engineered to be on the outside of the kick drum and swivel into place. Older style bass drums (as in my kit back then) slid from the inside out, and even at full extension about fifty millimetres or so remained in the kick drum shell. Bobby had accidentally hooked his trouser belt onto one of these and didn't have any room to free himself.

Eventually, Al stopped playing and came to the rescue. There was an embarrassing hiatus with me trying to keep playing with one hand, whilst hanging onto the offending drum with the other. Incredibly, a high percentage of the audience thought this was all part of the show, and when a ruffled Bob finally got himself free, with Alan's help, it was to massive applause as though Houdini had been released from his bondage. That was the last time, though. The great kick drum experiment was over.

In the van on the way home, I suddenly burst into hysterical laughter. There was no need to explain what I was laughing at. It broke the silent, sombre mood, and the others all began howling, too.

Neither Bob nor I were old enough to drive yet. We left that to Alan and Tony. Our old, blue Commer van was on its last legs, but we loved it. Proper bands drove around in a van, and as the mileage between gigs had increased, there was no way it would have been possible to play those dates otherwise.

Some nights when we weren't playing, we'd drive into town and cruise around, throwing a cigarette to any of the old fellers who lived and slept rough on the streets of London. Sometimes we would pull over for a short chat with them as well. We'd been gifted a huge American Stars and Stripes flag (I have no idea why or where it came from), which we hung on the outside of the van. It took up the whole of one side and was probably illegal, but we were never stopped by the Police. The flag caused some confusion about our country of origin, with bizarre conversations taking place between us and the rough sleepers. It was easier to lie to questions such as "How long are you here for" than explain the truth. We figured it wasn't hurting anyone, and a parting gift of a ciggy would be followed by "Have a safe trip" or "Say hello to the States from me".

The van had a number of eccentricities that I doubt would pass any MOT inspection today. They must have been more lenient back then about rust and minor defects than they are today. We could just about sit three in the front of the van, but anyone else had to travel in the back behind the bulkhead with all the guitars, drums, and general kit we carried. The van's rear door catch was dodgy. It locked from the outside with no problem, but from the inside, when unlocked, you had to be careful not to lean anything back against the door, otherwise it flew open easily.

Like most band members back then, we enjoyed some female attention. On one occasion a band member was in the back of the van with a young lady. Engrossed in the moment and locked in passionate combat, someone mistakenly leaned on the van's rear door and the inevitable happened. Fortunately, at the time we were driving very slowly up a London side street, and equally fortuitously at around two am, no traffic was behind us. In the front, the yell and the van door banging shut again could be heard above the engine noise. We stopped and swept up the resulting mess, with no lasting damage done other than some embarrassing grabbing of clothing and maybe a couple of bruises.

The band eventually split, and Bob fought on to release himself from the contract his parents and mine had signed on our behalf. We kicked our heels in and around Denmark Street in London, travelling up by train and hanging around the basement studios beneath Southern Music – a music publishing outfit run by Bob Kingsbury. Bob's son Barry was a record producer for the company, and we did quite a bit of recording down in their basement studio. Barry would suggest songs that had come the company's way for Bob to sing over. Sometimes I recorded drums on them, and sometimes not, if first choice session drummer Clem Cattini was around. Clem played on countless hit records and is still underrated for all the excellent work he did. By coincidence, he was in a band with Richard Hartley for a brief spell, too.

La Giaconda Cafe was a couple of doors down from Southern Music, and we would spend a lot of time in there, eating greasy food, drinking coffee, and hoping some influential music people would drop by, which they did occasionally. When we got bored, we would cross the street to Joe Macari's music shop and bother them for an hour or so. I can't remember ever buying anything in there, but Joe and his staff suffered us with good grace.

Having worked Denmark Street to death, Bob and I would try our luck in the music stores of Charing Cross Road just around the corner. I doubt we spent any money there either, although they knew us well and were always friendly. Our circuit would be completed by returning to the basement studio of Southern Music to hang out and see what was happening, until the last train back to West Drayton station had to be met.

All the while there was hope that Bob's contract might be brokered in some way. I went along, as a pal this time, to the same record company offices we had been to as a band, and listened to similar conversations and exaggerated promises as they were made again. It was a lazy, frustrating, hanging-about-waiting-for-someone-to-do-something time, and it couldn't last forever. I wasn't playing in a band now, and there were no short-term plans for Bobby and me to get something else going. He was waiting in vain, and I was doing my best to support him as a mate, but I needed to look after myself too and began to see if I could engineer something of my own.

Bobby's funeral took place in August 2022. We were in contact again for the last six or seven years of his life and spoke about meeting up, but it never happened. He was still bitter about the contract his parents signed, and his ill health (he had COPD – a lung condition) prevented him from singing any more. Given his talent, that must have been a frustration. After we broke up and all record company interest folded, he'd joined an Irish showband. I went to see them a half a dozen times or more, and they were a good, tight unit. He was earning a living, but it was hard graft and not what everyone had hoped for. As a member of the audience, watching Bob perform took me back to the very first time I saw and heard him sing. It was a joy. He moved on to minor success, and at one time was in a band with Canadian drummer Neil Peart, who was later in the band Rush. Bob was, without doubt, one of the finest vocalists I worked with. I'll never forget him and the fun we had growing up together.

Al and I met up again in 2018. He came to watch me play at a concert, and it was good to see him. He got a bit emotional that night, and we didn't have enough time after the gig to chat properly. The band and I had a long journey to our overnight hotel, so Al and I promised to meet again soon. He'd moved to

Devon, a place he loved, and died there unexpectedly a couple of years ago.

Tony, Al's lifelong friend, visited him many times in Devon and loved being with his best mate. Tony sadly died in 2014.

Mick went on to work in films, stayed living in London, and retained his love of music. I sent him a couple of my songs, and we wondered if we might try writing some stuff together. We spoke about meeting up next time I played in town. Mick died in October 2017.

That leaves me as the last man standing. I have no plans to die at all.

# CHAPTER 8

We had a short time off while the Classic Cinema was being converted into our new *Rocky* home. By lucky coincidence the weather was good, and I spent a few days away relaxing in the sunshine before the band reconvened to record the London Cast album at Sarm Studios. Sarm was part-owned by the actor John Sinclair, who'd been in the musical *Hair* with Richard O'Brien, and it was Richard's suggestion that we use John's studio to make the album. Sarm was indeed a fine studio, even though I didn't get to spend much time there. It took longer for me to unload, park, set up, and drink a cup of coffee than it did record the whole album, which comes in at just over thirty-seven minutes long.

I discovered early in the session that this was going to be a low budget recording when producer Jonathan King told me tape was expensive and he didn't intend on using much of it. Most sessions and recordings would keep more than one pass, or take, and then choose the best of those to work with, but that wasn't part of JK's budget-conscious plan. We rattled through the tracks one after the other, replicating note for note, beat for beat, what we had been used to playing nightly. As far as I remember, each track went down in one take, the first take, thus fulfilling JK's thrifty wish.

For those "more cowbell" aficionados (if you know, you know), I played the cowbell live on "Sweet Transvestite" exactly as I did in the show. There was only one overdub, which was on the song "Hot Patootie". I was asked to add a drum fill at the end of the track. They rolled the tape and said go. On the spot, without the chance to work anything out, I played the first thing that came into my head. Sometimes that works well – on this occasion it didn't – but such was the anxiety to move on, you can hear Jonathan shout over the talkback mic, "On to the next one!" before the track has even finished. On a remix many years later,

57

someone decided to deploy the good taste button and fade out the ending on "Hot Patootie". I didn't blame them and nor was I offended in any way. It was a bit of a relief.

Despite all its rough edges, the original album has great energy and accurately reflects the show as it was at the Theatre Upstairs. Smooth and polished it isn't, but I don't recall anyone suggesting or requesting we should aim for either. Punky long before the UK punk scene existed (and whose origin has been falsely attributed elsewhere), it was the music and fashion of *The Rocky Horror Show* which spawned the UK punk movement. It's always been a puzzle that it's never mentioned as an influence in either sphere, although it's obvious to me and others that it was. If nothing else, the show was the beginning of a more recognisably accessible and acceptable gender fluidity in a sexually repressed seventies society. All that from a ninety-minute piece of theatrical and musical fun, was some achievement.

The Classic Cinema Chelsea had first opened its doors in 1913. The decor some sixty years later I would describe as tired and fading. The building wasn't falling down; it looked to be perfectly structurally sound. Its fate, I assume, was down to its commercial value for redevelopment on a prime site in the Kings Road. In a few months' time it would be demolished and replaced by a functional, nondescript, money-making building, but its glory days weren't quite finished. It was to have one final hurrah when *Rocky* transferred there in July 1973.

I liked the Classic a lot. The building had warmth and a good feel. It wasn't better than the Theatre Upstairs – nothing could be; it was just different. The show was now on a bigger stage (literally) with more room for the cast to move around, which must have been a relief in many ways, but I wondered if a part of them missed the intimacy of the previous room in the way I did.

This time the band were on a specially built platform, stage right, which we accessed via a set of purpose-built wooden stairs. The view from up there over the audience was excellent, but the sound for the drums was awful. Where you position an instrument in any room makes a huge difference to the sound you get. Perhaps being so close to the ceiling and tucked away in a corner didn't work in my favour. I tried playing quietly, but still there were lots of overtones ringing around the theatre. I tried tuning up and detuning the drumheads, but nothing worked really well. In today's sophisticated world of theatre sound it would be different and solvable. Back then there was nothing more than adapt and work with what you've been given. In the end I did what I'd done as a kid trying to keep the volume down at home so not kill the neighbours. I threw a sheet over the whole kit. It may have deadened the sound a bit too much and there was less definition between the drums, but at least I wasn't overpowering everyone. Incidentally, it's how Ringo Starr recorded the Beatles' later albums – a tip he clearly borrowed from me. It's ok, Ringo, love and peace.

Once again, Brian Thompson and team had done a fine job. Those prophetic "Acme Demolition" tarpaulins hung around the walls reminding us all that this was only a temporary stopover. The lab was stage left on a scaffolding platform, almost directly opposite our own tower, and a trapeze had been installed there for Rocky to use during the Charles Atlas song. The ramp running down the centre of the auditorium was now many times its previous length. It enabled Nell to work up a real pace with Dr Scott's wheelchair and propel its occupant, Paddy O'Hagan, through the air (minus chair) and into the arms of Chris Malcolms Brad. There were a couple of times when I worried about Paddy's safety. Was he going to make the distance or not? Would the chair go off course, hit the side of the ramp and possibly turn over? Fortunately, nothing like that happened. It was a spectacular surprise and a nightly success.

After the Rocky, Rayner, glitter-down-the-pants incident, for the first time the show had two understudies – Trevor (Ziggy) Byfield and Angie Bruce. We had a new musical director too, in Brian Gascoigne (brother of Bamber, the much-loved host of the quiz show "University Challenge" on BBC television). Brian had been rehearsing with the cast, but it was decided that Richard H was to play the opening night and would relinquish the MD's chair after that. We had a new song to learn in "Eddie's Teddy", sung by the excellent Paddy O'Hagan in the guise of Doctor Scott. It was a straight-ahead rock 'n' roll number and came together easily, although I relied on my sheet music for a while as a back-up. Finally, with all rehearsals now behind us, we were ready to see what The Classic with an expectant full theatre was going to deliver.

This was to be Belinda Sinclairs first night, having replaced Julie Covington in the role of Janet. And huge credit to her, Belinda did brilliantly, as did everyone. The break had built even more anticipation amongst those who had read about the show or heard about it in some other way. That night was a triumph as by now we had come to expect. Everything went as smoothly as if there had been no break at all. The vitality, energy, and continuity between the Upstairs and this, our new home, was perfectly intact.

Our second first night party was an in-house affair at the Theatre. It was relaxed and easy-going, with everyone gathered in front of the stage. A bit like the Furniture Cave a few weeks previously, there were plenty of people I didn't know. They may have been the same people I hadn't known before. To balance that, a host of famous faces circulated around the room.

Well into the evening, and after we'd all had quite a bit to drink, someone said to me, "Do you know that Tennessee Williams is here tonight?" I'm not the most cultured being, but of course I'd heard of Tennessee Williams' *Cat on a Hot Tin Roof* and *A Streetcar Named Desire*. I knew them to be works of great literary importance by a classic American writer. I said in ignorance, "Christ, I thought he was dead" to which a little voice behind me said quietly, "No, I'm not." I turned, and sure enough it was the man himself. I was embarrassed and apologised, although he didn't seem to be at all upset by my remark. After that I surreptitiously watched him for a while. He didn't circulate around the room in the way I'd seen other well-known people do, and given the man's stature, surprisingly few people came to speak with him. He looked to be a bit of a loner, standing on the periphery, pursing his lips in a nervous silent whistle. Although I beat myself up for decades, today it feels like a badge of honour to say I insulted one of the United States greatest living playwrights in person.

The best and most comfortable seats at The Classic were in the middle of the auditorium. They were slightly bigger and more comfortable, and when friends of mine came it was those I always saved for them. None of the seats were numbered, and the uninitiated would rush to the front row, believing these would be the best seats in the house. However, halfway up the auditorium gave you the best view without having to twist your head around three hundred and sixty degrees, like a ventriloquist's dummy.

When David and Angie Bowie came with their entourage, they positioned themselves in about the right place. I didn't look for the Jaggers and wasn't aware if arriving so late meant they could even sit together. It didn't matter where Lou Reed and his leather-clad hombres sat, since five minutes after "curtain up" they all fell asleep until the show's end and then wobbled backstage to tell the cast how much they had enjoyed it. And so it went on, with seemingly the great, the good and the famous making their way through *Rocky*'s doors.

In order to satisfy demand, Michael White suggested we have a couple of midnight shows, ostensibly for those working actors in other West End productions who were unable to attend. I have no idea if that was unprecedented in the world of theatre, but it felt unusual to me. Michael proposed the extra shows would follow on from our usual nine o'clock performance, and we were asked if we would agree to this idea. It sounded like fun, and although from my perspective it was a physically tiring show to play, it was the cast who had to do the really heavy lifting. They all said yes, and a suitable financial deal was struck with little need for negotiation.

Next door to the Classic was The Pheasantry – a long running, favoured hangout for actors, musicians, and other such disreputable types. Today it's a Pizza Express, although they still have gigs down in the famous basement, and a few years ago I went back there to play one. I'm pleased it's survived, although the atmosphere is very different today. In 1973, with time to kill before the first midnight show, I decided to go somewhere for a quick drink. The Chelsea Potter was a pub we used further down the Kings Road, but that was subject to UK licensing laws. The Pheasantry was a club that closed when it felt like it and was literally on the doorstep. Time was tight; The Pheasantry it was. I'd been told the midnight shows would be by invitation only, and they would include mostly theatre staff and actors. I don't know if the actor Oliver Reed had an invite – somehow, I doubted it, as he seemed to be very happy where he was. I'd seen Olly a couple of times and I knew he liked a drink. He was in The Pheasantry again that night, not behaving badly in any way, just having a fun, inebriated time with a couple of his friends.

As I went to pass, he reached out a large arm and pulled me towards him. It was like being embraced by a cuddly Kodiak Bear. Olly was a happy and generous drunk. Sadly, it killed him in the end, and fittingly I suppose, he was in a bar at the time. By the way, those midnight shows were a huge success. The atmosphere was electric. The lateness of the hour helped, I think, and they felt like special occasions, a proper party.

As the latest additions to the cast, Ziggy and Angie's first roles were to work as Ushers pre-show and harass innocent audiences in any legal way they saw fit. Ziggy always had a wicked glint in his eye, and being given licence to roam the theatre and menace unsuspecting victims was a role he relished and excelled at. A scream or commotion from somewhere in the theatre told you an usher was about their business. A masked figure standing behind you or suddenly appearing over your shoulder was enough to cause a shriek of terror in most people. The ushers' inventiveness and sense of adventure grew nightly. It was good sport as long as you were a spectator.

I was on my way to the band stand one evening when Ziggy was patrolling along the front of the stage. I went to move past him, but he blocked my path. I moved to the left, and he to his right. For a few seconds we moved back and forth in a crazy two-man dance. The audience caught on straight away to what was happening, thoroughly enjoying my discomfort. In a whisper I said, "Ziggy, let me past, you bastard." He replied, "I don't give a fuck" and I knew he meant it. I had to either force my way past or play along and have some fun. I turned and walked away at pace, speeding up into a run, knowing he was almost certain to follow. I looked over my shoulder and sure enough we were on the gallop. This was going down well, as I ran around the theatre with Ziggy in close pursuit. I kept going, dodging deftly around people at the back of the theatre who saw us coming and sensibly got out of the way. It finally ended when I completed the circuit, reached the stairs of our band platform, and ran to the top. I turned to wait, not quite sure what I would do next, but Ziggy didn't follow and turned his attention elsewhere instead.

I'd enjoyed my debut performance almost as much as the audience had. It was fun, but I had no intention of repeating it. From then on, I was always wary walking through the theatre, especially when I knew Ziggy was on duty. Even the ushers' mates weren't safe.

I've never been star-struck, but there was one exception. Lauren Bacall, who was starring in *Applause* at Her Majesty's Theatre in London, came to the show. She sat on the very end of a row, roughly halfway up the auditorium, and appeared to me to be completely on her own. No partner, no entourage, just another anonymous member of the audience. Rayner Bourton in his book tells it differently. He says Angela Lansbury and Lauren Bacall were there on the same night, surrounded by their respective attendants, and that other audience members gawped in amazement. That's Rayner's recollection, but not mine. I didn't see Ms Lansbury that night (although she may have been there), but I did see Lauren Bacall from my perch on the band platform, before and during the show. No-one seemed to recognise her, or if they did then she wasn't stared at, bothered, or approached in any way. After the show, we spoke. As a kid I remembered watching her and other huge Hollywood stars on the tiny black and white TV set in the small front room of our house. It didn't seem possible that I would ever get to meet one of those stars. I know Ms Bacall had a reputation for being difficult. A bit of a diva some might say, a tough cookie. I imagine being a young girl in Hollywood in the 1940s you'd need a shell of cast iron to survive. She must have seen it all in an era of never to be repeated stardom. Speak as you find. I found her modest and very beautiful. I rang my parents the following day to tell them who I'd met – the only time in my life I did that.

We'd used a theatrical explosive device called a maroon at the Theatre Upstairs. They were detonated in a bomb tank which sat only five feet away from me. It was loud; very loud in that small room. I knew it was coming and covered my ears for protection, as did the other guys in the band, but the audience had no idea. And with the IRA's continued campaign of bombing targets around London, there were a few gasps, followed by nervous laughter, as the realisation set in that it was only a theatrical effect. We continued to use maroons at the Classic, although the bomb tank was under the stage, well away from us on our raised band platform. And now we doubled up and used two at a time. It was still loud but nothing in comparison to the Upstairs. As activity from the Irish Republican Army (IRA) intensified, I heard a few real explosions in and around town. They were all a distance away, but disturbing nonetheless. Some bombs were diffused, including one in December 1973 at Sloane Square Underground Station, about a hundred yards away from the Royal Court, although we had moved on by then.

We had two bomb scares at the Classic. It was easy for any hoaxer to dial the Police and say they'd planted a bomb somewhere. The Police assumed that most of those calls were a hoax but were obliged to take them seriously and turned up at our theatre on both occasions. The first visit was when we were well into the show. Derek, the house manager, came walking nervously down the central ramp and onto the stage. He didn't have a microphone, and in a quiet voice said something like, "I'm sorry, but we're unable to continue with tonight's performance." Apart from the front row, nobody heard it and wouldn't have known what was happening if they had.

A policeman at the back of the theatre was less ambiguous. He shouted loudly, "We've had a bomb scare. Please pick up all your belongings and leave the theatre quietly, while we conduct a search." There was no panic. The audience, also sensing this was a probable hoax, obediently filed out and we were asked by the Police if we would help. That started with us looking for any suspicious packages, until Tim very sensibly pointed out that if there was a bomb, we would be safer outside rather than not. That sounded like a good plan, so we left the professionals to it, and tumbled out into Markham Street via an emergency exit at the side of the building. This was where I parked my car every day in a parking bay where somebody (not me, but big thanks to whoever it was) had cut off the payment meter head. Everyone was too scared to park there, thinking they might be ticketed, so whatever time of day I turned up it was empty.

Here we were, the whole cast of *The Rocky Horror Show*, some (including Tim covered by his cloak, and Rayner in his glitter briefs covered by nothing) in full costume, huddled in a Chelsea side street. It wasn't the warmest of evenings to be in not much more than stockings and suspenders, so I offered my car as a refuge for anyone who wanted to use it. Had they all said yes, it would have been brilliantly funny to watch, but there were no takers. It wasn't that long until we were allowed back in, and Jonathan Adams restarted the show to loud applause. When we got to the maroons exploding, I did wonder what the reaction would be. It caused a commotion in the audience, but nothing more than normal.

The second time the Police arrived, I was much more blasé and didn't bother to leave the theatre. The cast stayed in their dressing rooms whilst a cursory search went on. We were soon given the all-clear and got back down to business.

Later, at the Kings Road Theatre, there was an accident involving the maroons, which spelt the end of their use. Our technician Roy was setting up for the second show after a matinee, and in his haste he had forgotten to close off the trigger switch. As he made the electrical connection to one of the maroons, it went off in his face. I was on the theatre balcony at the time and heard the noise. Belinda heard it as well and came rushing out of the dressing room guessing what had happened. We just looked at each other and couldn't speak. There was nothing to say. Roy was taken to hospital but sadly lost one of his eyes. We put on an extra late show one evening at 11.30, which was a sellout. All the money went to Roy, and it would have been a tidy sum but no real compensation for his loss. He returned to work after a long absence, but understandably the maroons were never used again.

The first cast defector (apart from Julie Covington) came seven weeks into the run at the Classic. Rayner had signed a shorter contract than everyone else and decided to go back to Glasgow and the Citizens Theatre. We were mates and spoke about it, but I didn't get this decision at all. I thought it illogical to leave the hottest show in town and everything that went with it, including a good salary, to return to Glasgow and likely obscurity. It had been a company effort to get us to this point, and I wanted that to continue, but Rayner refused to reconsider. And in the end, although puzzled by his decision, we all wished him well.

Our new Rocky was a gymnast, athlete, and all-round good guy, Andy Bradford. I hadn't been a part of the audition process, so my first meeting with Andy was at a full band and cast rehearsal. I liked him instantly and we got on well. His gymnastic prowess on the trapeze was impressive. Where Rayner swung back and forth not displaying many moves (well, one to be precise), Andy swung around the bar, performing tricks with strength and ease. Andy could hold a tune, certainly well enough for his part in the show. The rehearsals seemed to go well, but the problems began later when we got to the performance. Occasionally in "Sword of Damocles", Andy would start the song a little late and, having set off, wasn't able to pick it up again. There was nothing the band could do; it had to come from him.

The start of that song was down to me. I played four bass drumbeats as the count in, then the song went into the vocal immediately. There was no intro, no chance to ease yourself in for a few bars. On a platform on the other side of the full room from me, I truly believe Andy couldn't hear those four beats, and if he missed them then he was sunk. I kicked that drum as loudly as I could, and some nights it was fine, but not always. I tried to help by hitting the snare drum at the same time as the kick, increasing the overall volume further, but it still wasn't consistent enough. I know Andy was really uncomfortable with the situation, and I felt for him. Eventually he and the management agreed it wasn't working well enough and he left by mutual agreement. Although it's a cliched showbiz phrase, Andy went on to have a hugely successful career as an actor and stunt coordinator on dozens of TV shows and major films, including two James Bond movies. I saw him on TV a few times after he left, but never managed to catch up with him in person.

Three months passed quickly, and our time at the Classic had come to an end. It was the end too for the old cinema. As we moved out, the circling bulldozers began moving in. It had been a fantastic time in my second favourite venue. Swift work from Michael White, and the effort of Brian Thomson and team, ensured the momentum generated during the first five weeks of *Rocky*'s life had been maintained. The cast's talent and energy for every performance, plus a brilliant script, unforgettable songs, and Jim's direction, had made it an outstanding success. By now it felt as though there was no-one in London who hadn't at least heard of *The Rocky Horror Show*. Our final performance at the Classic was November 20th, 1973. I'm not sentimental about buildings, but it was sad to be leaving that place behind and then having the evidence of its existence completely destroyed.

# CHAPTER 9

So, we moved again. Our third venue was further still down the Kings Road, in an area known as World's End.

The Essoldo cinema belonged to the same group as the Classic, and for our purposes it was renamed the Kings Road Theatre, although nothing much internally or externally matched my idea of a theatre. It was a big, old lump of a building without any of the warmth or charm of our previous home.

The auditorium set-up was much as before. Some seats had been removed to accommodate the essential ramp, which ran down the centre of the building to the stage, with the laboratory on a platform stage left and Eddie's coke machine stage right. For the first time we had a band room (the equivalent of the cast dressing rooms) at the very top and back of the building. In a past life, it had probably been a storeroom of some kind. There were four hard chairs, a table, a fluorescent strip light, and no windows to the outside world. It had all the charm of a KGB interrogation cell, and for some reason we never used it.

The "bandstand" was situated at the end of a long corridor running down one side of the room. It had a waist-high wall, and to create the corridor, tarpaulins attached to scaffolding poles hung down on the auditorium side so that we were completely hidden from the audience. When we played, our little heads stuck up Chad-like above the wall so we could see and follow the action on stage. Once again, the positioning of the band was to suit the building rather than for any acoustic properties it offered. At least I could do away with the sheet over the drums and for the first time had some reinforcement with an overhead microphone and a monitor/foldback speaker beside me. It's impossible to say how such a basic set-up sounded to the audience. Theatre sound today is very sophisticated, and we would have been way off that mark, but it's possible with everything happening around them the audience didn't notice.

We had another new Musical Director in Frank Farrell. Frank later played bass in the band Supertramp and was a multi-talented instrumentalist. As a songwriter he co-wrote for many years with Leo Sayer, including their hit song "Moonlighting", which charted just about everywhere around the world. A further addition to the band was the excellent Phil Kensie on saxophone, who had played on the cast album we recorded at Sarm Studios. Phil eventually moved to the USA and has a list of credits to his name it would take too long to write down here.

There was one positive advantage to the band's positioning at The Kings Road Theatre. We were within yards of an exclusive emergency exit. Once the last chord had been struck, I would be out of that exit door, across the road and into the pub opposite, while the audience were still picking up their belongings and shuffling along the rows of seats towards the foyer. The increase in the pub's business was massive. It did so well from the show that they threw a private party for us. The doors were locked at closing time, all drinks were free, and after the first hour the bar staff gave up working. Then it became a boozy help yourself, all you can drink, Saturday night buffet.

A few weeks into the run, I made my usual exit from the theatre and was on a stool tucked away at the end of the bar, nursing a welcome pint of beer as usual. The theatregoers began to drift in, and before long I was surrounded by people who had just had the *Rocky* experience. As always, there was lots of excited chatter, and it was no surprise that Tim featured in every conversation. I didn't sit there deliberately eavesdropping on other people's conversations, but as they were taking place all around it was impossible not to hear some of what was being said.

I recognised the actor Charles Grey when he came in with his three male friends. They eased their way through the crowd until they were standing right beside me. I didn't recognise the other gentlemen, but assumed from their conversation they were fellow actors. They immediately began discussing the show, and there was no attempt to disguise how much they all despised it. Even Tim didn't escape criticism, which was a first for me.

Mr Grey said, "It's the beginning of the end of British Theatre when we have to endure rubbish like that." Everyone in his party agreed wholeheartedly, and another round of drinks was followed by more vitriolic comment. It wasn't something I'd heard until now, but equally, what did it matter?

I didn't mention it to anyone in the cast or crew; there was no reason to do so. The sold-out theatre and the audience reaction every night spoke for itself. Those guys were the toast of the town. It was many months later when I heard that Charles Grey was to play the part of the criminologist in the film. I was stunned and amazed to learn he was prepared to be a part of something he despised so much. I imagine his scenes in the film were shot separately, and I guess being paid for a few days' work overcame any doubts or principles he may have had. Charles Grey claimed repeatedly to never having seen *The Rocky Horror Picture Show*. I'm sure that's not a lie. He didn't claim to have never seen the show, which wouldn't have been the truth. His performance in the film was massively inferior to Jonathan Adams role as the narrator, and I always wondered what he said to those drinking pals after accepting a part in a show they all hated so much.

I would occasionally visit the theatre during the day to pick up an item for a recording session, for some maintenance on my kit, or just because I was passing. On a couple of those visits, auditions were taking place, with Frank Farrell accompanying the hopefuls on piano or guitar. If there was time I'd stay for a while to keep Frank company and watch the actors going through their paces. At times it could be toe curling, but I had to admire the courage and self-belief of the people up there. It was something I would have been unable to do. One memorable guy must have had the only theatrical agent in town who didn't know what *The Rocky Horror Show* was about. His audition piece was "There is Nothin' Like a Dame" from Rogers and Hammerstein's *South Pacific* – a choice unlikely to make the right impression in an audition for Rocky Horror. He was dressed in the full American sailor's outfit of white hat and T-shirt over blue trousers. He sang well enough, albeit in a phoney American accent, and when asked to do another song of his choice, more in keeping with rock 'n' roll, said he had nothing prepared. I followed him out of the theatre and watched as he jauntily made his way down the Kings Road, still in costume. He looked happy enough but wasn't offered the role.

# CHAPTER 10

## 1969

"Drummer Wanted" said the advert in the weekly music paper *Melody Maker*. The small print didn't make any of the usual extravagant claims, so I rang the number, auditioned a few days later, and finding we suited one another, I was in.

The band were about my age and lived and rehearsed in Ealing, West London, which was an easy drive from home. Dave Mansell, Peter Bennett, and Laurie Mellor were all friends from Ealing College who had been gigging around London for some time, playing a healthy mix of good original songs and quality covers. Frontman Peter Bennett had a knack of getting gigs and the confidence to approach anyone he felt could help progress the band further. There were meetings with some of the country's best known musical executives, like Phil Solomon. Big Phil had a successful roster of artists, strong links with Decca Records, a financial interest in Radio Caroline, and ran his own label, Major Minor Records. I'd been in this situation many times and listened with cynicism as he went through his routine, making all the right noises, saying all the expected things. *Deja vu*; nothing came from it.

In the end the band got management with Tokenam Aw, henceforth known as Tok. Tok lived in a classic London mews house, with its own pub at the bottom of the small street of trendy, hugely expensive properties. In the evening a polite gentleman stood guard to stop non-residents' cars driving into the mews and parking up for the pub. "I'm here to see Mr Aw" were the magic words that always got me past Mr Security, making me feel superior as I swept through in my rusty Ford Anglia estate car.

I had no idea how Tok got his money, nor was it my business, but he seemed to enjoy a fine lifestyle. I didn't know if he was either any good or got by on charm and cheek, which he had in abundance. It didn't matter; he was doing a fine job and got us a meeting with the NEMS record label, run by Clive Epstein – brother of the late Brian, who was of course The Beatles' manager. Clive, who had taken over the family's NEMS empire, was a quiet, down-to-earth guy who didn't bother with all the verbal nonsense and exaggerated promises we'd heard previously. That meeting resulted in agreement to record and release a single under the NEMS record label. The band were renamed "Now" to give us a contemporary feel, and a recording session was arranged for a couple of weeks' time.

We had some band photographs taken and were assigned a publicity lady called Angela, to help with press and all things promotional. At the end of our second meeting, Angela asked if I could give her a lift home, which being a helpful sort of person I was happy to do. Angela was probably in her early forties (I didn't think it polite to ask), I was nineteen. She had a small, elegant flat and didn't seem to mind having a rusty Ford Anglia parked outside on multiple occasions.

"NOW" recorded a song written by Peter Bennett called "Marcia", which was released as a single. It wasn't very good, got a small amount of airplay, and deservedly sunk with the rapidity of a large, weighty anchor. The B side was "The Hands of My Clock" which along with guitars, drums, and piano, had a string quartet playing on the session, scored by Richard Hartley. Richard was a tall, quietly spoken guy from Yorkshire, with a cool persona and a mass of curly hair which exploded very impressively from his head. I wasn't to know then, but over the next few years Richard was to feature a lot in my musical life. The release of "Marcia" coincided with an unexpected gig at The Royal Festival Hall, supporting Fairport Convention, compered by the Radio One DJ John Peel.

Angela had worked some magic, and at the last minute we were added to the bill. The Fairport lineup included Sandy Denny, Richard Thompson, and drummer Martin Lamble, who was tragically killed when the band's van crashed on the M1 Motorway. Strangely, I've crossed paths with Fairport many times since, including two appearances at their own Cropredy festival, without ever being close, nor mentioning the Festival Hall gig. Fairport were very impressive at that concert, with innovative, well-crafted songs, beautiful vocals from Sandy Denny, and fine musicianship all round. Arguably, at that time they were at their height, although two classic albums followed with Dave Mattacks now taking over in the drummer's chair.

Our lack of sales meant NEMS weren't keen to repeat the NOW single experience, and gradually the band's interest in playing gigs together began to wane. It was a slow winding down of operations, and I started looking around to see what else might be musically possible. Before I got involved elsewhere, Peter Bennett came to the house to show me his new acquisition – a beautiful, twelve-string Martin acoustic guitar. We played around with some new songs he was writing and trying out some harmonies. During a break, and just for fun, he played me the first song he had ever written aged eleven or twelve. "The Seagull's Name Was Nelson" was a true story of being on holiday with his parents and finding an injured seagull. It was extremely corny, but for a lad of eleven or so, not a bad piece of work.

Later in the evening we rang Tok to update him on what we'd been doing. His answerphone kicked in, and instead of leaving a sensible message, for fun we sang a verse and chorus of "The Seagull's Name Was Nelson" down the phone then hung up. The following day Pete got a return call from Tok. Unbelievably he said, "That song. I love it. I want to record and release it as a single." Peter explained it was a childish piece of musical naivety. "Mart and I were having a bit of fun, Tok, there's no way I'm going to record that." But Tok was immune to all resistance and insistent that it was a potential hit song. "I'm taking it to RCA later in the week," he said.

Not believing RCA would be daft enough to be interested, Peter said, "Okay, I'll leave that with you", hung up, and instantly rang me to share the joke. Like Peter, I couldn't see how anyone would consider that song to be a commercial proposition. I said, "So is Tok taking his answerphone into RCA to play it for them?" On every level the idea was absurd.

Four days later I got another phone call from Peter. "He's done it," he said. Who's done what? "Tok! He's got an agreement with RCA to release that bloody song as a single and negotiated an album deal to follow." There was a pause on both ends of the phone while this sunk in, then Peter continued, "I've got a meeting with RCA next Wednesday. That song is an embarrassment."

This was an extraordinary piece of news. The record company that had signed Elvis, Diana Ross, and David Bowie wanted to release "The Seagull's Name Was Nelson" after hearing thirty seconds of a recording on an answerphone. It confirmed my belief that record company executives knew absolutely nothing about music. I declined the offer to attend the meeting – it was none of my business – but understood Peter's dilemma. I said, "Look, I know it's surreal, but you have to go to the meeting, and if they're prepared to give you a decent deal then take it."

The contract was duly signed, and whatever reservations some of us had, Peter, Tok, Richard Hartley, and me, along with a session standup bass player, assembled in a studio in 1970 to record "Nelson". The drum kit was only required on the B side – a track called "Magic Picture Wall". Someone (presumably Tok, lovely man though he was) decided to add a choir to both tracks. It got weirder. The Co-operation choir, a mix of men and women around thirty-strong, pitched up to be on the recording. As the name implies, they all worked at the Co-op (an organisation that ran a series of food shops, insurance agents, and undertakers, amongst other things). During the day the choir members stacked shelves, worked on the tills at the Co-op, and for all I know were funeral directors. For them it was exciting and a great day out, making a record in a proper recording studio.

Nothing about that record pleases me, and I know Peter felt the same way. The irony is, thanks to all the record pluggers and the promotional budget from RCA, his very first song was the most successful thing he ever wrote. Tony Blackburn was a Radio One DJ with an influential daytime show. "Nelson" was his record of the week, an accolade and piece of promotion that usually ensured a top twenty hit. It got masses of airplay on BBC's Radio One, not just on Tony Blackburn's show, and Peter along with the choir appeared on television's Top of the Pops. I declined to join him and play congas on camera (protecting the little street cred I possessed), although I went along to watch the recording. "Nelson" reached number forty-five in the charts, which equates to around thirty-five thousand single sales. It was covered later by a couple of other artists in Europe, and my guess is it made Peter a few pennies, but knowing how record companies operate I wouldn't count on it.

We did some gigs on the back of the "success" of Nelson, after which Peter went off to play some solo concerts. Eventually, we reconvened at IBC's studio in Portland Place to make the album and follow-up single. Once again Tok was in the producer's chair and Richard Hartley the arranger for those sessions. Lots of great records had been made at IBC. The Kinks, The Who, Elton John, The Bee Gees, and many more, had all recorded successfully there. The live room was accessed by a lift for heavy equipment like drums, or several flights of stairs when you were feeling energetic. It was a spacious room, more than big enough to accommodate an orchestra, with a good feel and fine natural acoustics. The control room, with a set of windows facing down onto the live room below, was accessed from the studio floor by a set of wooden stairs, very similar in layout to Abbey Road.

John Pantry was our excellent in-house engineer for the whole album. Once all the drum tracks had been put down, I didn't need the lift to come and go any more and used the stairs instead. The building next door to IBC was the Chinese Embassy. From the stairwell it was possible to see clearly into a couple of the sparse offices, where uniformed Chinese officials sat at their desks with nothing but a telephone, paper, and pen in front of them. It was voyeuristic but I couldn't resist stopping for a few seconds to look in every time I went past.

This was the era of Chairman Mao, when China was an even more mysterious closed and secretive society than it is today. The Communist Party ruled with a ruthlessness that was completely at odds with the liberty and freedoms that my generation and much of the Western world enjoyed. The official never looked up from his work, although he might have sensed I was watching him from only five yards away. Often, those cheeky Chinese Embassy chappies would transmit messages back to the motherland. It was usually early evening, but it could happen anytime of day. Their transmissions interfered with the recording equipment at IBC and meant we had to wait until they were finished sending before we could carry on. It was frustrating and expensive (thankfully, I wasn't paying) if you were in the middle of something important like recording with an orchestra and halfway through a good take. It wasn't as though you could pop round to the neighbours and complain, although it might have been fun to try.

The traffic in London in 1970 was bad, but still much lighter than it is today. Luckily, I always managed to find a parking space, day or night, within easy walking distance of the studio. On this day, I'd parked up and was strolling back towards the IBC building roughly two hundred yards away, when a side door of the Chinese Embassy opened and a young man in a suit, not a uniform, came out, took a photograph of me, and shot quickly back inside again. It was completely unexpected and puzzling. Why had he done that? I started to wonder if the official I'd watched many times from the stairwell had seen me after all and considered my behaviour warranted some kind of investigation. Was there a list of suspicious looking drummers who needed to be kept on file and monitored for potential activity detrimental to the regime?

I'd been coming in and out of the IBC building for weeks, at times during the day, sometimes at night. I can only guess that for some reason I'd been marked out, or the young guy was a music fan and had mistaken me for someone else. The former seemed more likely. Many years later, I read the MI5 officer Peter Wright's book *Spy Catcher* and discovered one method often used to bug buildings of interest was for people posing as workmen to place listening devices by drilling through the wall of an adjacent building. It was a crude but common practice apparently and might have been possible with IBC and the Embassy buildings being so close together. Whatever, I quite liked the idea of being considered subversive enough to be checked out by the Chinese authorities. Maybe there's a file somewhere gathering dust with a picture of me strolling down Portland Place with a smile on my face.

*The Ballad of Galdwain* was released on RCA Victor in 1971. Making that album at IBC was a good experience. Everyone involved was a pleasure to be with, and I learned a lot about recording and even more about production and mixing. Producing isn't a precise art, and arguably there's no such thing as a bad mix. It's all very subjective, time consuming, creative, and great fun. I attended every session and mix at IBC. Maybe I became a bit of a nuisance, an unwanted presence always lurking in the background, although nobody ever said anything. If that was the case, I'm totally unrepentant. I loved every second and was eager to learn in a top-class studio environment with people like John Pantry. We recorded a follow-up Peter Bennett single at IBC called "Catch the Summer", which was also released on RCA in 1971. Although far superior to its predecessor, it received very few plays on radio, which was a pity since with a similar push, or even a minor one, it could have been more successful than "Nelson". Such is the fickle and transient world of pop music.

After our time together making the album, Peter moved on to do his own thing and I picked up again with Barry Richardson, another Ealing resident who played bass, sang, and had good contacts in the live music scene. As well as working together, Barry kindly recommended me to a couple of other outfits as someone who could be relied on to do a decent job. One of those was a Country band called Jan and the Southerners, who had an American female bass player when Americans were rare in London and female musicians rarer still. I wasn't a big fan of traditional Country music, but my bandmates were good people, the gigs were fun and paid well. They included a number of American Air Bases scattered around the country. The Gi's were an enthusiastic audience and, aside from the money, artists were always well looked after, with plenty of food and drink available throughout the evening.

Sticking to tradition, I took my dad along to one of those gigs. I hadn't given a thought about whether gaining entry into a sensitive air base might be difficult. When I pulled up at the barrier, a large figure came out of the darkness and shone a torch into my face through the open car window. I explained I was the drummer in the band playing that night. The soldier grunted acknowledgment and shone the torch across to the passenger seat.

"And who's this guy?" he asked. Now I was slightly worried about whether we would both be able to get into the gig. I couldn't lie and say he was a member of the band, so I said rather weakly, "He's my dad." The soldier lightened up and laughed. "Ah, ok, so he's your dad. How you doing, feller?" he said, shining the torch back to the passenger seat. My dad smiled back rather nervously and said in a typically British way, "I'm very well, thank you." The soldier gave us directions, opened the barrier and waved us through. God Bless America. I love Americans.

Barry also introduced me to one of his visiting friends from the States. The very English Ian Whitcombe. Ian was a fascinating character. Actor, singer-songwriter, author, producer, presenter, and a few other things to boot. In 1965 he hit number eight on the Billboard Hot 100 with a composition of his own, "You Turn Me On", sung in a breathy falsetto voice. Ian had made the record when studying at Dublin University, and he travelled to the USA during a break in the academic calendar, where he appeared on numerous TV shows, played The Hollywood Bowl with The Beach Boys, and then toured the States with The Kinks and The Stones. All of that during a summer break; it was extraordinary stuff.

Ian had a slight stammer when he spoke, which fortunately wasn't there when he sang, and his follow-up single "N.E.R.V.O.U.S." reflected that speech impediment. Recorded when he was in Hollywood, "NNNNNervous" reached number fifty-nine in the billboard charts, before Ian returned to Dublin to complete his degree and graduate with a BA in History. As if all that wasn't colourful enough, in 1969 he produced an album for Mae West, *Great Balls of Fire* for MGM records. It didn't sound like the easiest of jobs. Mae West was seventy-eight years old and had to be helped into the studio, then propped up close to the microphone to record those album tracks. Good on her, though, she was a game gal to the end, a real trooper. Despite not having hits in the UK, Ian was a cult figure to a few well-informed music-loving bikers, and they turned up to see him at most of the gigs we played. The Hollywood Bowl it wasn't, although Ian didn't seem to mind, and I knew no different.

Playing piano at those venues, Ian attacked the keys with a ferocity and madness reminiscent of Jerry Lee Lewis. With Barry on bass and me on drums, we rocked our way through those gigs, and although most took place in well-worn establishments, they were all enjoyment on a stick. One surreal moment was in a rough old boozer on the outskirts of London. Ian suddenly switched to ukulele, climbed onto a table in front of the stage, and sang "The Eggplant That Ate Chicago" to a pub full of leather-clad bikers: they loved it. Eventually, Mr Whitcombe returned to America where his home, family, and diverse career were all based. I heard from him periodically, and he came back to the UK from time to time for work and to catch up with old friends.

I last saw him presenting on TV, wearing his journalistic hat on "The Old Grey Whistle Test". Sadly he passed in 2020 from complications after a stroke he suffered in 2012. He was busy writing and working up to the end. Barry Richardson was another who passed way too early. In 1971 Barry formed Bees Make Honey. It was a timely move with the pub rock scene in full productive flow and the band did really well, building a good reputation for playing live then getting signed to a deal by EMI. Had I still been around it's possible I might have been asked to play drums. Instead, they recruited American gun-for-hire Bob Siebenburg, or Bob C Benburg, or Bobby C as he became known. Although it's painful to admit, Bob was a better player than me and proved the perfect fit for Barry's band. In the small musical world of coincidences, he went on to play drums for the band Supertramp with my *Rocky Horror* musical mate Frank Farrell on bass guitar.

While Barry was forging ahead with his project, I was studying with the National Youth Jazz Association in Highbury, North London. NYGA was a great organisation where, for a nominal fee, you got fine tuition for all jazz instruments, including drums. The sessions and lessons took place at Highbury College. In one room saxophones worked next door to trombones, while in a third trumpets trumpeted, and so on. Sometimes walking down the corridor, a cacophony of instruments all playing together sounded like a free-form jazz ensemble. There were ample opportunities to form small bands from those classes and bigger bands, too.

I played in lots of trios and big bands where, somehow, I adopted an Irish mate, Shaun, who played trumpet, albeit with more enthusiasm than technique. He was good for my ego, though, as he continuously told me what a great player I was and how it was a privilege for him to be in the same band as me. I made the mistake of giving him my phone number and, lovely guy though he was, Shaun would ring up at any old time and I'd be part of a one-way "conversation" for a good hour or more. On one occasion, having started on a subject, I put down the phone, walked to the kitchen, put on the kettle, then went back to the phone. Shaun was still in full flow, so after squeezing in a couple of yeps to let him know I was there, I returned to the kitchen to make the tea. He was such a good-hearted lovely guy, I didn't want to upset him by saying, "I have to go now, mate." So instead, I took to ringing my own front doorbell, which I made sure he could hear. After using this ploy four or more times, he said, "Jeez, you're a popular fella. Always people coming round. Still, I'm not surprised. See you's." And he was gone... until the next time.

In The Recording Studio

This was taken during a dress rehearsal.
Tim Curry, with my drums just visible behind the screen

Frank Farrell. Backstage at The Kings Road Theatre

Dennis Cowan. Backstage at The Kings Road Theatre

Mum and Dad

Crims People, left to right: Tony, me, Mick, Bobby (seated) Alan

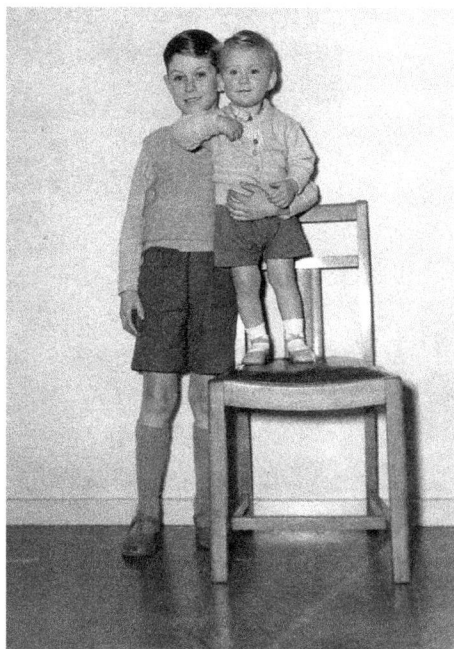

Big Brother Paul and Me

Now, Promotional Poster, left to right: Laurie, David, Peter and me

CQ Hug Backstage. Me, Gerry and Nick

Nell's Mask and My Hat

The Infamous Red Testicle

**The Theatre Upstairs**

**ROYAL COURT**

Royal Court Theatre Sloane Square London SW1
Telephone 01-730 5174-9
Telegraphic Address Engstaco London SW1

President The Earl of Harewood
Chairman Mrs J Edward Sieff
Hon Treasurer Mrs Kenneth Snowman
Hon Secretary Mrs Pauline Matthews

To. Martin Fitzgibbon Esq.,                    31st May, 1973
26, Lavender Rise,
West Drayton,
Middx., UB7 9AW

Dear Martin Fitzgibbon,

   This is to confirm that you will rehearse and play the music
for The Rocky Horror Show by Richard O'Brian at the Theatre Upstairs
at the Royal Court.

   The engagement will commence on Sunday 10th June, and the
show opens to Previews on 16th June and to the Press on 19th June
playing until 14th July 1973. The performances are at 10.00 p.m.
Mondays to Fridays and at 11.00 p.m. on Saturdays. It is understood that you will be on first call to us for the period of the
engagement for rehearsals and up to eight performances per week.

   You will be paid a fee of £100 for the engagement, in five
installments of £20 each. It is understood that this fee covers
the hire and transport of your instruments.

   I enclose an information sheet about the Theatre Upstairs and
I look foward to meeting you in June.

                              Yours sincerely,

                              Harriet Cruickshank
                              Manager

I agree and confirm the above.......................Date..........
                              (Martin Fitzgibbon)

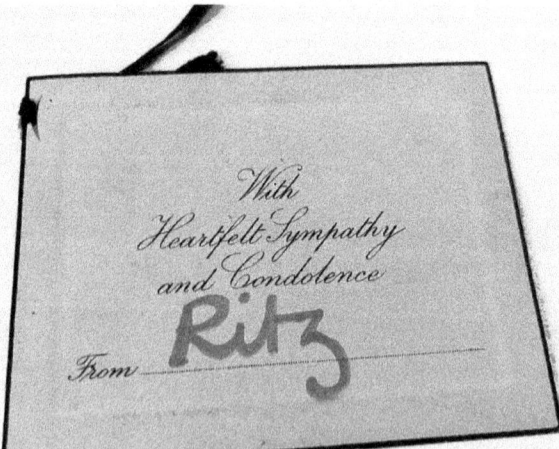

*With*
*Heartfelt Sympathy*
*and Condolence*

From _____ Ritz _____

My Contract and First Night Card

The Dockery Boys. Derek Rutherford, me
and Mark Cole, at a radio station

The Jigantics with two interlopers. Left to right, Mark Cole, Stan
Laurel, me, Olly Hardy, Sarah Kelly, Barb Granger, Keith Thompson

# CHAPTER 11

It would be hard to find two more opposite personalities than Keith Moon, drummer with The Who, and Dennis Cowan, our bass player in *The Rocky Horror Show*. Where Keith was wild and outrageous, Dennis was quiet and reserved. Although an unlikely pair, they'd become mates when the Bonzo Dog Band and The Who toured the States together in 1969.

Keith first came to see the show at The Kings Road Theatre with his girlfriend, and Dennis introduced me to them in the pub afterwards.

We had a couple of drinks then Keith, who was always restless, suggested we move on to a place he knew. It was post-show on a Saturday night and tomorrow was our day off; it seemed impolite to refuse. We went to a club, then after a brief stay, on to another, Keith's well-known face giving us instant access everywhere and lots of attention (not all of it healthy) at each stop. Our last call was a party, a longish drive by shared taxi.

The party was in full swing when we arrived, and although my head had been getting fuzzy for a while now, I hung in there for a respectable amount of time, before eventually shutting down completely.

It was around two o'clock on a Sunday afternoon when I woke up on a comfortable sofa in a very large house. There must have been plenty of bedrooms, but I hadn't made it to one of those. Although I didn't like the idea of being the person who falls asleep on the sofa at a party, it was too late to be embarrassed. I set off in search of a bathroom, and after very cautiously opening some doors, discovered a downstairs cloakroom. From there, finding the kitchen was easy, and in the first large, American-style fridge I'd ever seen (looking like a monster sitting in the corner) was the milk I needed for tea. This house was absolutely huge. I knew it didn't belong to Keith, and there definitely wasn't a Rolls Royce parked in the swimming pool.

I was nursing my mug of tea in the kitchen when a lady housekeeper appeared. She wasn't in any way fazed or surprised by my presence and kindly offered to make me some breakfast. I settled for honey on toast, and while she busied around, asked if she knew of a local taxi.

"Yes," she said, "we have someone we can call who's very reliable and discreet." I smiled at the discreet bit, which in my case wasn't necessary, and asked if she could try and arrange something. I wanted to go pick up my car and get back home to shower, clean up properly, and have a change of clothes. Mrs Housekeeper made the call, and twenty minutes later a private car turned up. As it was a Sunday, we spoke about a price. It wasn't a negotiation; I asked, and he told me it would be forty pounds, which sounded reasonable, and I had that in my wallet.

It had been a long day and a short night. I wasn't feeling great, nor much like talking, so I asked if I could sit in the back, thinking I might sleep for most of the journey. I tried, but Mr Taxi was reeling off a list of famous people he'd picked up from the house and delivered to places in and around London. He cheerfully dropped names and bits of gossip about famous people I didn't know but had certainly heard of. So much for the diplomacy then. Having temporarily run out of steam and anecdotes, he asked what I did, and I replied I was a journalist; a showbiz correspondent working for the *Daily Mirror*, looking at stories for a new weekly gossip column the paper was launching. I said it in a light-hearted way, but he wasn't sure if I was winding him up or not. He went very quiet just in case, and finally I got some peace and time to myself dozing in the back of the car.

My girlfriend shared a house in Fulham with three other girls, and ten days or so after the party, I was driving from her place up the Kings Road, on my way to the theatre. Up ahead I could see a commotion of some kind. Then as I got closer, I realised it was Keith. He was on the pavement shouting and throwing stones at the passing cars. Luckily, he needed to reload and was searching for fresh ammunition as I went past.

I guess Keith could be multiple personalities depending on what he might be "on", and being an adventurous type, he would try pretty much anything, including (allegedly) at an infamous gig in the USA a handful of horse tranquillisers swallowed down with brandy.

It was tragic but not a huge surprise that his life ended early, given the indulgence and the lifestyle he was afforded. My memory is of a guy with a huge appetite for fun and a wicked sense of humour, whose celebrity allowed him to indulge in excess. You couldn't help but like him, most of the time.

Some members of the *Rocky* cast enjoyed donning an usher's mask and jacket to help terrorise the hapless audience preshow. I understood the appeal. There can't be many opportunities where you could indulge yourself in anti-social behaviour without running the risk of being arrested. Being an usher wouldn't have worked for some of the cast, but others like Nell snuck out front when the mood of mischief took them. I'd been up in the balcony at the Kings Road Theatre, and as I came through the door into the auditorium Nell's mask was on the floor in front of her and the look on her face was one it's impossible to describe. She was in full makeup, hissing with fury, like a wild cat protecting her cubs. As she stormed back to the dressing room, I went over and picked up the mask. I didn't want the person who'd torn it off to have a trophy of some kind. There was minor damage to the eyelet and the elastic was torn at the side where it had been ripped off Nell's face. I literally threw it into my drum case, closed the lid, and forgot about it. It stayed in that case for the next twenty or so years. I didn't intend to keep it as a memento, but all this time later I still have it.

I hadn't seen what happened, nor who was responsible. It was only a couple of years ago I discovered it was the singer-songwriter Cat Stevens (now Yusuf) who was the culprit. I shared a festival stage with him some years ago, before I knew he'd behaved like an arse. He was a bit of an arse then, too. It's unlikely that I would have kept a mask from the show under any other circumstances, so I guess I have to thank him for that at least. It's a rare piece; probably the last original one in existence.

I couldn't give you an exact date when it happened. The best I can do is say with certainty it was 1974 when the show gradually began to morph into something else. Suddenly we were on the tourist route. Coaches would pull up outside and drop busloads of Japanese visitors, who would file in quietly and patiently to take their seats. The Japanese understand theatre. It's part of their culture, as is politeness, and they would sit and listen with no response to anything during the performance. If they understood the dialogue or any of the action, they didn't show it. The entrance of Frank, the birth of Rocky, Eddie appearing from the fridge; everything passed in silence. At the end of the show, they would applaud with polite restraint, file obediently back to their buses, and spend the night in some corporate hotel on the London outskirts before taking in Hampton Court or Stratford on Avon the following day. Other tourists were on the loud side and clearly enjoying themselves, but I wasn't any longer. It was the right time for me to move on but stupidly I didn't.

Where early audiences got references to Fay Wray and Charles Atlas, much of the dialogue now seemed to go over people's heads. Phrases from the narrator like "It was clear this was going to be no picnic", no matter how well delivered, had zero impact where previously they'd raise an audible laugh. If you can sense the beginning of the end of something, then this was it.

It was also the beginning of a new beginning, and fifty years later the show survives and thrives. Today it seems the audience are as important as the cast. People dress as their favourite characters and have created their own dialogue. There are shadow casts and audience participation that mirrors a pantomime. Some are living their fantasies and secret desires; others are just having a fun party night. The weird one is me, not them. Whenever I think of the show, I remember how it was with the original cast at the Theatre Upstairs. That's how it works best in my head where none of us have aged a day, and nothing has changed at all.

All of my time with the *Rocky Horror Show* coincided with a very difficult period in my life. I don't want to dwell on that, but it helps to explain what happened next.

By 1974 I was completely emotionally shot, although I foolishly failed to diagnose it. A relationship I cared about deeply and fought hard to preserve had finished. I carried on working hard, thought I had recovered a little, and after a time drifted into another relationship with Mel. It wasn't on the same level as before, not even close, but sharing time with someone who cares about you and giving something in return is a healthy human condition.

Mel had the chance to improve her career in hospitality, which meant a positive step up and a move down to Cornwall. I wished her well, and beautiful though Cornwall is, I felt it wasn't the right time for me. Mel and I were never going to be life partners; we both knew that and parted on good terms as friends. We packed all her things in the car, mostly clothes and plenty of kitchenware, then drove down to Cornwall for the start her new life.

Mel seemed to settle in quickly and was enjoying the new challenge in Cornwall. In contrast, life gradually began to take its toll on me. The show was always the most important part of my day. Everything revolved around the performance and me being in good shape to give it my best. Now as showtime got closer, for the first time ever, I began to get real nerves, a kind of stage fright. One of our old stage crew, a lovely guy called Bill, once told me how having trained as an actor he had to quit through stage fright. Up until now I'd always found that idea puzzling, but no longer. The minute we started playing, everything was fine, but for the hours preceding, it built up until I was literally shaking with nervous exhaustion. Matinees were the worst, as I had to go through preshow nerves and the shakes twice. On those days (Fridays and Saturdays) I would walk down to the Chelsea embankment between shows. There was a bench in front of a statue where I'd sit trying to relax and rationalise what was going on in my head. The walking and fresh air helped but didn't make anything go away.

The most sensible decision I'd made for years was to take a break from the show, thinking a holiday would get me back to something like normal. Mel down in Cornwall was the obvious choice. We'd spoken on the phone a few times and I knew she was settling in and doing well. I wasn't trying to reignite our relationship, but it would be good to see her, and I thought perhaps showing me around her new surroundings would take my mind away from everything else. She had helped me through my lowest point and would either tell me off or more likely put an arm around my shoulder to offer a healing solution and sound advice. I rang her number and a male voice answered. I didn't speak and put the phone down. Cornwall wasn't going to be an option. A needy ex-boyfriend turning up wasn't going to work.

Instead, I drove to Aberdovey on the Welsh coast. I walked through the village, past all the painted houses – a feature in many Welsh seaside places – then onto the beautiful but incredibly windy beach, hoping that wind would blow all the nonsense out of my head. I hadn't booked anywhere in advance, found a decent hotel but only stayed one night and then moved on. There wasn't a plan after that. I drove a bit, looked around during the day and would find the best hotel I could to spend the night.

I've never minded being on my own, but this time solitude wasn't helpful. The only people I spoke to were at garages filling up the car, hotel reception staff booking me in, and waiters taking my order for food. I probably cut an odd figure sitting at a table for one, looking miserable, not eating very much and then disappearing to my room. I never stayed anywhere more than one night. I was unhappy and depressed, but with no show looming there was zero pressure, no shakes, and that was a big positive. After a week away I was back at the theatre. My dep was a young, good-looking guy with an enviable mass of curly hair who was mad keen to play the show and had badgered me to let him do it. He came in around three times, to sit beside me and make notes of the cues and little extras required. I rewrote some of the drum parts for him to reflect the minor changes made over time.

When I got back to the theatre, my bandmates and some of the cast told me quietly that they'd missed my playing and they were glad to have me back. Two of the female understudies said they were going to miss my dep, but for a different reason. The day after I returned, so did the tension and all the uncontrollable nerves. I knew I could do this show. I'd done it a thousand times. All I had to do was stop my head from malfunctioning, turn up and play. But telling myself that and doing it, was now becoming impossible.

Even amongst the chaos, there were some moments of light relief. It's a tradition amongst UK theatres to have a cat, and at the Kings Road Theatre we had one, too. I can't recall his name, I'm not sure if he even had a name other than Cat. You'd see him very occasionally during the day, but that was rare. I'm an animal lover but it was hard to get up close. I guess Cat was a bit shy like me, and as soon as the audience began to assemble, he was away backstage, or wherever theatre cats disappear to during their time off. Part-way into a show one night, Phil Kensie who played Sax noticed something was going on in the audience. I couldn't see the audience from my seat, but we could hear a bit of an unusual commotion coming from the other side of the tarpaulin that divided us from them. We'd poked a peephole or two on the tarp just around where Phil stood, and he peered through to find out what was going on, then began to beckon us over. The cat must have been chasing a mouse, and in the thrill of the hunt had overcome any reticence to enter the auditorium. The pursuit was on.

We followed the progress by the screams and jumping around in the seats, as something unexpectedly brushed around their feet and legs. I'm sure a few people thought it was another aspect to the show, and had we been able to replicate it nightly it would have been a winner. It was like a variation of the children's game "Splat the Rat"; you could never tell where the action was going to pop up. It would be quiet for a few seconds, and you wondered if that was it, until there was a sudden rumpus in another section of the theatre. "There he is!" one of us would point and shout, as silently as it's possible to silently shout. It was a one-off performance, at least in my time at the Kings Road Theatre, and the end of my time was fast approaching.

I struggled into "work" one day. It was a Saturday and matinee. I had somehow got through the two shows on Friday and managed to drive in, although it had been difficult. And to add to the other symptoms, I now had a physical pain in my side which was spasmodic but painful when it kicked in, like a knife being jabbed into you. Part of my OCD (as it would be called today) was a fear of being late and letting people down. I always arrived early at the theatre, and today was no exception. When I got to the band area, the only person around was Monica Brophy, one of the stage management team. I'd gotten this far but suddenly knew I couldn't do it. I can't explain why not. I knew I wouldn't be able to play the show that night. The whole of my body seemed to be shaking, the stabbing pain in my side was happening more frequently.

I was reminded of Bill, the crew member at the Theatre Upstairs, who'd told me all that time ago how stage fright had "forced" him to run offstage. For the first time I knew exactly how he felt. I wanted to run, to be anywhere but in this place. I said to Monica, "Look, I'm really sorry but I don't feel well. I can't do this. I've got to go."

A psychologist told me years later that animals fall into two categories when cornered. It's commonly called flight or fight and is the automatic reaction to an event perceived as stressful or frightening. The perception of threat activates the nervous system and triggers a response, preparing the body to fight or flee. I'd been fighting this thing for months and now I was finally done, beaten into submission. I didn't say anything else, just turned and left as quickly as possible. My fighting was over; I was fleeing. On the way out through the foyer I kept my head down, feeling ashamed, and didn't pick it up again until I was back at the car I'd only recently parked. My first sense as I drove away was one of massive relief. I didn't have to go through that painful preshow ritual after all. About a half mile up the road, I pulled over. I couldn't see to drive anymore.

The next morning, I got a phone call from Monica. I guessed the call might be coming, but instead of asking if I was okay, her opening line was hostile. "It's Monica. You let us down last night," she said. "That can't be allowed to happen again."

I was taken aback. I considered Monica a friend, not a close one but a working colleague I'd shared a drink with on many occasions. I had never missed a show or rehearsal before, never been late for either. Against doctor's orders I'd played shows and Monica knew that. Now on behalf of the management she couldn't even ask if I was okay or needed help of some kind. My reply was brief. "It won't happen again," I said. "I quit." And I put the phone down.

A couple of hours later I drove to the theatre. It was empty apart from someone sitting in the box office. I nodded to them as I went into the auditorium and down to the bandstand. I packed all my kit into its cases, drove the car to the side door emergency exit I'd used countless times before, loaded up, and left for the final time.

Of the three venues I played with the *Rocky Horror Show* the Theatre Upstairs remains my favourite. That was the most creative time. Everything that flowed and followed in other venues with other cast members over the next 50 years and counting, draws on a legacy which came from that place. In a different time, it's possible that a small experimental show might have completed its three-week run and disappeared without trace. They say timing is important for the success of any endeavour. I'm convinced that's true. 1973 was very different to today. With hindsight, it provided the perfect social and creative conditions for the emergence of a show like *Rocky*. To borrow a sporting phrase, Richard O'Brien had timed his run to perfection, and London in 1973 was ready for something different and refreshing. *Jesus Christ Superstar* and *Godspell* had sucked up the musical oxygen of Christianity. The American-led musical *Hair*, with its post-Woodstock ethos and calculated box office nudity, seemed to have run its course. Like a herd of charging rhino, up the centre aisle of a tiny London theatre came *The Rocky Horror Show*.

Those who made it all possible, in no particular order:

Sue Blane, the brilliant and unassuming costume designer had previously worked with Tim Curry at the Citizens Theatre in Glasgow. The "Citz", as it's known, featured in many of the *Rocky* cast's theatrical history. Sue, who was awarded an MBE in 2007, was almost solely responsible for creating the template of punk fashion in the UK – something that took far too long to be recognised, having been unjustly bestowed upon Vivian Westwood. Ms Westwood did nothing to refute that accolade, aided and abetted in the deception by her partner Malcolm McLaren. The couple had a clothes shop on the Kings Road a short stroll away from the theatre and were known to have visited the show on more than one occasion, absorbing and being influenced by what they saw. There's nothing wrong with emulation and adaptation; it can be equally creative. But the failure to acknowledge any influence or the source of your inspiration is disingenuous and deceitful. Mr McLaren has never acknowledged the musical influence that *Rocky* had on him and the UK punk scene either, although it was apparent to those of us involved at the time but appears to be oblivious to lazy researchers and musical commentators, too.

I didn't see much of Sue at the theatre. Most of her work had already been done by the time we got into deep rehearsal. Sue would quietly arrive from time to time (she is a quiet person) to make a small adjustment to a costume, or produce a piece procured from somewhere or other. She'd stay for a while to watch as the developing action unfolded and disappear as silently as she arrived. One day she handed me a top hat to wear which had been sprayed with glitter (a lot of glitter was used back then). I still have it. The glitter has faded, but the hat is fully intact and is otherwise in pristine condition. All the band wore them and an usher's facemask during the big reveal at the end of the show. After the Theatre Upstairs production, the band were no longer hidden from the audience and the idea had to be discarded, which was a pity. I enjoyed the theatricality and artistry of the final twist to an already surprising show.

Little Nell (Nell Campbell), who played Columbia in the stage show and in the film version of *Rocky*, is a force of nature. There was a definite antipodean presence in the show. Nell was originally from Australia, as was director Jim Sharman and set designer Brian Thompson. Richard O'Brien, born in Cheltenham, moved with his family to New Zealand before returning to the UK in 1964. Nell arrived with her family from Australia in 1970 and had a stall in Kensington Market, selling clothes. Opposite her on the market, selling footwear (boots mostly), was Queen singer and frontman Freddie Mercury (whatever happened to them?) who Nell says constantly reminded her about his band and talked up their impending success – something she treated with great scepticism. Along with displaying her tap-dancing skills busking on the streets of London, Nell worked at Smalls, a cafe in Knightsbridge, when the two Richards and Jim Sharman came in. She obviously impressed and was hired that day to play the part of Columbia. Nell wasn't the world's greatest tap dancer, but the dance sequence in "Time Warp" was a space created specifically for her.

I was asked by Richard Hartley to supplement the tap by using my sticks on the rim of the snare drum. It wasn't written on the original score, and I'm not sure if the idea came from Jim, or one of the Richards. But it seemed to work, and as no-one objected, including most importantly Nell, I assumed it was ok and kept it in. Nell ducked out of the show after seven months when it was close to the top of its game but rightly returned to take part in the film. She owned that part. Later, in New York she and her partner, Keith McNally, whom she first met at the Kings Road Theatre, opened a nightclub called appropriately "Nells", which was hugely successful and became the place to go and be seen in the Big Apple. There's a great picture of Nell, Bob Dylan, Andy Warhol, and Sting, together around a table in the club.

Nell was signed to A&M records from 1974 to 1978 and released a handful of songs co-written by Richard Hartley and Brian Thomson. Eventually, most of the *Rocky* antipodeans moved back to their homeland, including Nell, who returned to the boards in 2022, and as I write is touring her own one-woman show.

Nell and Pat Quinn have an informal double act at the *Rocky Horror* conventions around the world. Those fans who didn't see the original production might be unaware that Pat opened the show as an usherette, complete with ice cream tray slung around her neck, and sang "Science Fiction Double Feature" (sung in the film by Richard O'Brien), which she did with huge charm and perfectly in character. Audiences loved her; she was incredibly cute, and all the men and most of the women would have been happy to wrap her up and take her home with them.

In the usherette role Pat had to sit quietly and stock still under a piece of white muslin as the audience filed into the tiny room that was the Theatre Upstairs. She didn't move a muscle and it wasn't evident if she was even breathing under there. Then once everyone was seated and showtime commenced, Pat emerged like a butterfly from the chrysalis to perform the show's opening song. I was told by Richard Hartley that Marianne Faithful – actress, singer, and arguably best known as a former girlfriend of Mick Jagger – was being considered for Pat's role. For whatever reason, it didn't happen. Perhaps Marianne didn't fancy sitting under a muslin cloth for fifteen minutes or thereabouts; we will never know. But for me, a Magenta played by anyone other than Pat Quinn would be unthinkable.

Born in Belfast, Pat was yet another actor who performed at The Citz theatre in Glasgow. For a while she worked as a blackjack-dealing bunny at the Playboy Club in Mayfair. I played in a band at the Playboy Club around the same time, but it's unlikely – although not impossible – we would have met. Between sets the musicians were only allowed in the Bunnies' canteen, where free food and soft drinks were served, whilst a conveyor belt of stunning Bunnies passed through. It was a tough gig, but we stuck with it. Having married the actor Sir Robert Stephens in 1995, Pat became Lady Stephens, which is probably extremely handy when booking a table at a restaurant.

Paddy O'Hagan, who played Eddie and Doctor Scott in the original stage production, had been a founding member of the Pip Simmons theatre group. Paddy played saxophone, which he did on "Hot Patootie" – his number as Eddie in the show. As Paddy tells it, at his audition he and Richard O'Brien had jammed a bit, with Richard on piano and Paddy on sax. At the end of it they discussed a shared interest in B movies such as "It came from Planet X". Then as Paddy went to leave, he said to Richard, "Well, good luck with it", meaning the musical and thinking he hadn't made a significant impression. Richard then asked if he wanted a part in the show, to which luckily, he said yes.

I liked Paddy a lot. He and his wife Jude were very kind to me. Understandably he has been somewhat eclipsed by Meatloaf, who took the role of Eddie in the film. In both his roles, Eddie and Doctor Scott, Paddy was excellent and his contribution to the show's success has been underestimated only by those who never witnessed it. It emphasises one more reason why the *Rocky Horror Show* was a success. The whole cast were terrific.

Tim Curry graduated from the University of Birmingham with a BA in English and Drama. Some of the *Rocky* cast were actors who could sing a little rather than primarily singers who might act. Tim clearly could do both. He had the voice, along with a stage presence to match, plus the ability to sell a song. Tim shone throughout rehearsals, always wearing those women's shoes to keep him in character. There was only one opportunity to see his entrance for the first time, and I clearly remember mine. Then I got to watch everyone else's first experience from a privileged viewpoint behind the screen facing the audience.

One of many great moments of the show was to witness Tim throw off his cloak to reveal stockings, suspenders, and corset, whilst belting out "Sweet Transvestite". It's a great song, and the marriage of the image, Tim's singing, and the song itself, was extraordinarily powerful. Tim knew of the Theatre Upstairs from being in the production before *Rocky*, called "Give The Gaffers Time to Love You", which wasn't a huge success. It didn't put him off going back, though, after he'd read the script given to him by Richard O'Brien. Asked about his first reaction to the dialogue, Tim said, "It was fun, funny, witty, and original, and I thought, 'If they get this right, it will be a great big hit.'" They did, and it was.

*Rocky* rightly made Tim Curry into a star overnight and ultimately a world star, which the film was responsible for. But the film wouldn't have happened had it not been for the show. It was obvious from the first day of rehearsal that this role was perfect for him. Despite the names touted for the film, including Jagger and Bowie (something repeated often but I have never believed), there was only one person who should and, in my view, could play the part of Frank. Before our first night show, when I arrived at the theatre there was an envelope sitting on my snare drum. Inside was a "break a leg" card from Tim. A nice touch. When he left to go to the States to open *Rocky*, I returned the gesture with a card of my own. I was sad to see him go. It was another break in the chain of the original cast, and I knew he would be irreplaceable.

Like Sue Blane and Tim Curry, Rayner Bourton spent a couple of seasons at the Citizens Theatre, Glasgow. Rayner and I would often meet prior to the show in the pub next door to the theatre. Pre-rehearsal and show drinks were confined to non-alcohol so not to cloud whatever we were about to work on. During one afternoon break in dress rehearsal, Nell came bursting through the door of the pub to find us. It was an arresting entrance. She was resplendent in full makeup and vivid costume, including spangly pants. We were so used to seeing her like that it seemed perfectly natural, but the rest of the pub's clientele were visibly startled by this red-haired whirlwind in full flight.

A few days later, I was relaxing in the same pub when Rayner came bursting through the same doors. On the way to the theatre his car had run out of petrol in The Mall, a road which leads up to Buckingham Palace. The Irish Republican Army (IRA) were carrying out a number of car bombings in London in 1973/4, and the Police were sensitive to any abandoned vehicles, in particular those close to a Royal Palace. We jumped into my car and got there in record time to find the vehicle being cautiously observed at a distance by several Police officers who were waiting for an Army Disposable Bomb squad to turn up. The Army's preferred method was a simple one of blowing up the suspect vehicle. On our rescue mission journey, my suggestion to Rayner was to let them blow the car up, then claim on the insurance. My plan was flawed when Rayner confessed to not actually having any insurance.

Rayner played the role of Rocky with a distinctive Brummie (Birmingham) twang, adding to the comedy and irony of a created creature having such an unlikely accent. The opening to his song "The Sword of Damocles" started with the voice rising from bass to tenor as his bandages were unwrapped, repeating the line "The Sword of". The final layers had him physically turning around, until having reached peak falsetto and before Rayner collapsed in a giddy heap through lack of oxygen, Richard Hartley would signal me to play four kick drums beats which led us all into the song.

Chris Malcolm was born in Scotland before his family moved to Canada, where he attended university before returning to the

UK. Chris's North American accent was authentic in his role as Brad Majors. Although he never considered himself to be a singer, Chris made a fine job of his song "Once in A While" on the original London cast album. His vocal delivery of that track showed a sensitivity and fine interpretation of the lyric and melody. It's one I remember recording at Sarm Studios, because I had to quickly switch from playing tambourine to brushes. And as everything was going down live to tape, Richard O'Brien stood by my drum kit, handing me the brushes to play the rest of the track. I'm pleased that on the recording the transition sounds smooth. In my opinion Chris would have been great in the film version and should have been cast. He remained connected with *Rocky Horror* for decades after becoming a director of the "Rocky Horror Company", which was established for the show's first West End Revival in 1990. As co-producer and occasional director, he was responsible for mounting hugely successful touring productions of *Rocky Horror* in dozens of countries around the world, for almost 15 years.

Richard O'Brien was cast by *Rocky* director Jim Sharman in *Jesus Christ Superstar*, and perhaps more tellingly in Sam Shepard's *The Unseen Hand* at the Theatre Upstairs. Shepard is cited by some as having a profound influence on Richard's writing and subsequent success with *The Rocky Horror Show*. I'm in no position to judge. All I can say is I've been influenced by so many people in my musical life that if I collected them all together, they could fill the Albert Hall. Sadly, that doesn't mean I have the ability to write songs or make records that come anywhere close to those incredibly talented people. Everyone has their influences, subliminal or calculated in a plagiaristic way.

I don't believe Sam Shepard could have written "Time Warp" or "Sweet Transvestite". Nor as an American would he have understood the British perspective or irony of some of the script. Writing successful dialogue and songs that stand the test of time or just capture the mood of the moment is a very tough thing to do. If you don't believe me, give it a try. I wish you luck. A few people query if Richard had any help in the writing of the show. Music, lyrics, and book are all solely attributed to him. I don't have any inside knowledge to share with you. What I can say is in my experience a good music producer can make a huge difference with suggestions, ideas, and minor alterations to a song. Tweaking stuff is easy when the basics are already in place. The hardest challenge is having the initial idea and bringing that to the table. I know Jim suggested a title change from Richard's initial "It Came From Denton High" to *The Rocky Horror Show*, and I'm sure some tweaks from Jim and possibly members of the cast helped the process. But there's no doubt in my mind that Richard was the creative force.

Julie Covington, the original Janet Weiss.

Julie had appeared in *The Adventures of Barry McKenzie* alongside Chris Malcolm. I had seen Julie on television before we met, and I was aware that she was performing songs written by two other names I'd heard of – Pete Atkin and Clive James. I wasn't blown away by the songwriting (sorry, chaps, just my opinion), but I recognised the quality of Julie's voice. Appearing on television didn't translate into Julie being difficult or different to everyone else. She was grounded and lovely. The popular version, at least on some internet sites, is that Julie was badly injured during a dance routine with Rayner and was then unable to continue with the show. I've even read that she was hospitalised, which is complete nonsense. Julie was accidentally hurt. She hit her head on a concrete pillar during a dance routine with Rayner, which would have stunned anyone, but she never missed a beat and finished the song without many people knowing what had happened, including me, and I was six feet or so away.

Julie couldn't continue with *Rocky* as she was contracted elsewhere after our allotted slot of five weeks at the Theatre Upstairs came to an end. She came to see the show at The Classic. I spoke to her afterwards, and I know she enjoyed seeing the performance for the first time from an audience perspective. She said to me, "This is great, and the show works incredibly well here." She was right, of course. It did work at The Classic, and after the confines of the Royal Court would have been a relief for the cast to spread out and not be tripping over each other.

I don't know if she had any regrets about leaving and not being a part of the Classic cast. Only Julie could tell you. She went on to great things, including a number one single with the Rice and Webber song "Don't Cry for Me Argentina", later turning down the role of Eva Peron, as Julie considered Peron to be an unsavoury character. That was typical of her and hugely to her credit. More success came with the television series "Rock Follies", and the song "Only Women Bleed" reached number twelve in the UK singles chart. After the run at the Theatre Upstairs, Julie was followed in her role as Janet Weiss by Belinda Sinclair, who as I've already said was terrific and ensured a seamless transition.

As well as being an actor, Jonathan Adams was a fine artist with a taste for surrealist cartoons. He trained at Chelsea College of Art and exhibited many times throughout his life. Jonathan was forty-one when he joined the cast, making him the elder statesman of the company. I remember him looking a little lost sitting with his wife Julia in the stalls at a Theatre Upstairs social event. There was no intent to isolate him nor any division in the company that I was aware of, just a difference in age. Jonathan was a lovely guy, and as I've said before, brilliant in his role as the Narrator. That lugubrious quality he brought mirrored nicely the Edgar Lustgarten figure I had seen on TV and whom Richard O'Brien had based the narrator around. At our first meeting his character was so memorable that it was the one I took away with me. Jonathan departed the show on February 19, 1974, and went directly into rehearsals for *A Tooth of Crime* by Sam Shepherd, which was being staged at the Royal Court. It reunited several of the original cast and creative team, including Brian Thomson, Jim Sharman, Richard O'Brien, Sue Blane, Richard Hartley, and Christopher Malcolm.

I was delighted he was in the film (as Doctor Scott) but will forever regret that his narrator role – and in particular his time warp moves – wasn't committed to celluloid for all the world to see. The deep baritone voice you hear on the original London cast recording is his; yes, he could sing, too. The final exhibition of his artwork took place at The Riverside Studios just a couple of months before his death. His role in *Rocky* was big another factor in its success and a wonderful piece of casting.

Jim Sharman, Director. Jim was born in Sydney and into the world of travelling sideshows, showbiz, and circus, via his dad who ran Jimmy Sharman's Boxing Troupe in Australia. Jim was slight and not especially tall. I couldn't imagine him following his father's sporting example in the tough world of Rugby League or boxing, but you never know about the quiet ones. He directed in a calm and measured way. I never heard Jim raise his voice to make a point or issue an instruction. Instead, he gave off a sense of quiet authority which meant you knew who was in charge and who had the final say.

Unlike most Aussies of that era who were drawn to London in the late 60s seeking adventure and/or career opportunities, Jim was already a huge success in Australia. He was specifically chosen by Rice/Lloyd Webber to be imported over to London to direct *Superstar*, because they were so impressed with the original Australian production which he had just directed (and Brian Thomson had designed). Jim graduated from a production course in Sydney in 1966 and of course went on to direct *The Rocky Horror Picture Show*. We nicknamed him "Cloggy" in an affectionate way. I never saw him without his authentic heavy Dutch clogs adding to his distinctive walk, with arms swinging and thumbs upraised on both hands. His attention to detail became obvious during rehearsals, although if he had an opinion about anything musical, it came to us via the correct channel of the Musical Director Richard Hartley.

Brian Thomson was the scenic designer and long-time collaborator with Jim Sharman. They had met in Australia at the Old Tote Theatre company in 1969. Like Jim, Brian was quiet and quietly spoken but with a more pronounced Aussie accent. I didn't see much of Brian. I guess most of his work with set design had already been done. He and Jim were a close team and would quietly converse on occasions about minor alterations to the action.

Brian did an amazing job with the set design at the Court. Somehow, he crammed in a host of ideas into a room that size. His subsequent work at the Classic Cinema, *Rocky*'s next venue, and to a lesser extent at the Kings Road Theatre was also spot on. In 1996, Brian won the Tony Award for Best Scenic Design for *The King and I* on Broadway and received an Order of Australia

(AM) for services to the arts. His archives are held by the Australian Performing Arts Collection, which gives you an idea of his importance and prolific output.

Other equally important people: Gerry Jenkinson and Peter Hunt lighting; Marion Kernahan, Alkis Kritikos, Chris Peachment, Hilary Cruikshank, and my bandmates.

# CHAPTER 12

1974

My hobby for the next year-and-a-half was sleep – something I became very good at. Sleep was a welcome friend, a warm and comforting companion when it arrived. There were times when I asked whoever might be in charge to let me carry on sleeping. That would have been a perfect natural solution rather than a manufactured one, which had been under consideration, but ultimately rejected on the basis of those left behind are the ones who suffer most.

I'm happy all these years later that those middle-of-the-night pleas were ignored. I would have missed so much; life is a beautiful gift.

Like Humpty Dumpty, I tried to put myself back together, but when there was no improvement I sought help from outside. My local GP, who generally was a decent man, hadn't offered any medication nor explanation to what was happening. The inexplicable stabbing pain I'd had in my side had almost disappeared, but my broken-down head still played up massively. Frustrated by me not responding to the "pull yourself together" prescription, the good doctor lost his temper one day and angrily said, "I can't help. You better go and see a psychiatrist."

I heard those words with a mixture of fear and relief. Fear that I was truly mad and might end up institutionalised (something that troubled me often), but relief in that I would have seen anyone, including the local witch doctor or snake oil salesman, had it made a positive difference.

An appointment was duly made at the local hospital to see a Mr Gleed. He had the appearance of a professor, with a mass of coarse hair in a very low side parting that swept from one side of his poorly disguised bald head to the other.

Having briefly assessed this creature in front of him, Mr Psychiatrist referred me to one of his female colleagues, a psychologist, who at a later appointment opened up proceedings by showing me some ink shapes on paper. A gentleman called Hermann Rorschach developed this test back in 1939, and today it's largely dismissed by the trade as being old-fashioned nonsense. I was way ahead of the curve and those experts with my own assessment. Every time I was shown an inkblot and asked what I saw, I replied truthfully – it's an ink blot! Not completely deterred, the psychologist moved on to photographs and asked if I identified with anyone in the picture. I genuinely welcomed help, that's why I was there, but I had to be honest and said no. Perhaps then, she suggested with a hint of impatience, I could make up a story about a child in one picture? What might they be doing or thinking in that scenario? The picture was of a boy looking wistfully out of a top floor window of a large house, into the garden below. I had a reasonable imagination, and it was easy to come up with a story about a child, possibly at boarding school, waiting for his parents to pick him up. They were returning from India and on their way home to a house in the country. Or, I said flippantly but in a deadpan way (there weren't many laughs in those days), he might just be watching and waiting for the milkman to deliver so that he could have his breakfast cereal.

The lady nodded, but I noticed didn't write anything I'd said down. She asked if I felt a great sense of personal loss. That was an easy question to answer. "Yes," I said, "everything that was important in my life has gone." Finally, what did I think about this consultation and psychologists in general. Based on this brief experience I said, "I don't get any of it. I don't believe in the ink blots, or the pictures." We agreed to differ but were able to affirm that there was no point in making a further appointment. Her assessment, she said, would be sent to my GP. I thanked her and left with a sense of relief and minor disappointment. On the upside, no men in white coats had suddenly appeared with a straightjacket to hustle me away, but I felt no further down the road to recovery than before. The result of her consultation, as reported to my GP, was "severe depression". I didn't need confirmation of that. It was something I knew much better than anyone.

Skulking miserably behind the drawn curtains of my flat wasn't getting me anywhere, so I forced myself to go out to places I found restorative and peaceful. Good friends did what true friends do and rallied round to help in any way they could, although I still had my moments which they tolerated with patience and understanding. Then surreptitiously a thin veneer-like layer of self-confidence was added piece by piece, day by day, week by week until I gradually felt alive once more.

I have no idea how long it had been – possibly two years since I'd departed the *Rocky Horror Show* – before I decided it was past time to kickstart my life and do something. Having earned no money for so long and lived on savings, an income of any kind would be useful. Plus, if I was able to hold down a job, I knew my attention would be focused elsewhere, and with that hopefully confidence would continue to grow.

My drums had been stored away, and there was never any thought of getting them out again. Not for a moment did I consider it possible for me to do so. I can't explain why, I guess I just couldn't deal with the painful idea of playing any more. That kit went with me on three house moves but remained in its cases. It would be something close to twenty years from the time I closed the lid on those drums at The Kings Road Theatre until they once again saw the light of day.

One of the jobs I'd done while trying to make a living in music was working for an electrical wholesale company. I started in the stores and was quickly asked if I would run the goods inwards department. Next, came the trade counter, and finally the office asked if I would join them on the sales desk. How's this for a coincidence? I was on the phone trying to chase an outstanding order with the London office of a company called Walsall Conduits. The switchboard put me through to the relevant department, and the voice that answered the phone sounded very familiar. I didn't say anything straight away until I was certain it was Richard Hartley, who was also trying to make enough money to survive while waiting for his musical break. That was then, in my pre-*Rocky Horror* days, and here I was now with my musical life behind me.

The local paper ran an advert for a storeman in an electrical wholesalers. It was something I had experience of, so I went for the interview and was hired. There's a dignity in having a job, a feeling of self-worth that is overlooked and undervalued by those responsible for hiring, firing, and shaping the lives of others. I'd come almost full circle, pretty much back to where I'd started. The money wasn't great, but having a place to be every day at a set time gave me a purpose to get up in the morning.

My new workplace was far from glamorous. The office space was placed over in one corner, partitioned off with chipboard. The warehouse was basic, too, with no facilities except a kettle for making tea. We used the toilets in the unit adjacent to ours. There were three of us, plus a driver, in this new branch, which meant I had to muck in and do a number of jobs. I was expected to look after the stores, goods in and out, serve customers on the trade counter, and answer the phones when the other guys were tied up. Sometimes, when they went out, I did all of those simultaneously. Six days a week I was kept busy; most pleasingly I had no time off sick, and a year and more passed easily enough.

I still hadn't kicked the habit of drifting into jobs without applying for them. One of the guys moved on and I was asked if I would like to become a sales representative for the company. Between ourselves (don't tell anyone) I wasn't bothered. Indifference is never what any boss wants to hear when they offer you a job. They want you to be hungry to succeed and willing to go to any lengths to climb the slippery ladder of success. That isn't me, but I admit to being seduced by the company car, expenses, and a big jump in salary. I probably should have said no thanks, but instead I said yes, which historically was typical. I never seem to learn.

This new job involved selling, and I wasn't a natural bullshitting salesman. Had I been selling something like vacuum cleaners, door-to-door, I doubt I would have lasted a week. As it was, I started by looking after a few existing accounts, and deliberately not trying too hard sell them anything worked. It was a kind of reverse salesmanship. I found by not being pushy, but honest and helpful, people responded favourably. I had to bring in new customers as well and ultimately would be judged on the sales figures I generated, but adopting the same approach worked there, too.

It was around this time I began socialising again. John and Jennie Butler were good friends who had a kind of open house, and lots of people gathered there particularly at weekends. There were many parties, where I always arrived alone and left the same way, which I'm sure was the subject of some discussion and puzzlement. Eventually, though, I formed a relationship with Sarah – the youngest of three sisters I knew. In retrospect it wasn't a match made in heaven. In fact, it was much more than that and a huge mistake for us both, but hindsight is a wonderful thing. Sarah went off to study in Paris. They say absence makes the heart grow fonder, and it may have been that day-to-day distancing which helped to keep it together. We got engaged, which seemed a good idea although it really wasn't. Sarah was moody and very difficult at times, and those times were frequent and became more and more prevalent. I put up with it. I'm incredibly stubborn and rarely give in when I believe it's justified. However, when we had disagreements it would be me that backed down and smoothed things over. Having taken so long to enter another relationship perhaps I was desperate to keep this one alive and glossed over what was patently obvious to others and should have been to me.

The beginning of the end came when I picked her up at the station on the way home from Paris. As I got out of the car to greet my fiancée, she fired off a volley. "What are you doing?" she yelled angrily. Startled, I thought I was doing what most people would have done. I imagined after a few months apart that a small sign of affection, a hug at least, would be appropriate. Perhaps I should I have sat in the car, let her lift that heavy suitcase into the back, and shaken her hand in greeting once she'd got in.

We broke up very soon afterwards (instigated by her, of course), and only then did Sarah confess that in those moments of lost temper and abuse she would push me as hard as possible to see if I would break, and when I didn't, push me further still. Would I take it? How far could she go to test my resolve? It was an extraordinary callous admission to make to someone you once purported to love. It was partially my fault, though. I let her get away with too much too often and she took advantage of that. Abusive bullying behaviour isn't stopped by turning the other cheek, and most disappointingly of all isn't confined to the male of the species.

Friends rallied round once more. "Thank goodness you're out of that relationship," they said. "It was poisoning you." Now that it was over, I finally realised it was the truth. No-one leaves a serious relationship totally unscathed. It hurt, of course, but thankfully not on the scale I'd experienced previously, and the realisation I was better off made a huge difference to my recovery time.

To say I got headhunted makes it sound more dramatic and me more noteworthy than is the truth. An American lighting firm called Edison Halo had promoted one of their area managers, Roy Langley, to national sales manager, and Roy asked if I would take over his old area, covering London and the Home Counties. Lighting appealed to me in an artistic way, and a number of ethical issues with my current job had been bothering me for a while. It was time to move on, and after getting past the interview with the Managing Director at Edison Halo, I was hired.

Roy took me to meet all the clients I was to look after, and they included some real characters. On day one of the job and our very first call, we drove into London and up the Caledonian Road. Known colloquially as the "Cally", it's a long road by London standards, approximately a mile-and-a-half, with a mixture of retail shops and houses. The north of the Cally is the more affluent area, and the south houses Pentonville Prison and runs down to Kings Cross Railway Station. The lighting company was run by a pair of business partners known affectionately as the Cally Boys. Roy parked the car as close as possible to the shop and, suited and booted in our finery, we began walking up the street. Up ahead, I could see a commotion, which turned out to be the Cally Boys having a water fight on the pavement outside their shop with buckets full of water being thrown over each other, then racing back inside again for refills. It was an interesting first day and introduction to my new job. Whenever I visited those guys, something always seemed to happen.

The Cally Boys had a retail and wholesale business, with the shop at the front facing onto the Caledonian Road. It served an eclectic mix of local people. Anyone who has worked in retail will know that dealing with the public is challenging at times, and like a moth to the flame they found their way through the door of that shop. Verbal sparring happened on a daily basis, and on one occasion a fist fight was about to break out between a customer and staff member over a trivial remark that had escalated and gone wrong. As a spectator and noncombatant, it was interesting but somewhat uneasy entertainment.

On average for Edison Halo, I would make five calls per day, which I considered good going through the London traffic and finding a place to park. With the Cally Boys it wasn't unusual to write off the whole day and sometimes night. I took them and two of their employees out to lunch in an Italian restaurant, a place they had suggested and where they were well known. Lunchtime spilled over into afternoon and then early evening. The waiters kept on bringing us double brandies, and after I'd drunk at least six I tried concealing them behind menus and on the empty seat next to me, anywhere I could. But hiding didn't work. The waiters, seeing no brandies on the table, just kept bringing more for me to try and stash somewhere. Drink driving laws were relaxed back then, but with the wine during the meal and the brandies following it, I wasn't in a proper state to drive anywhere. Having seen the boys off in a taxi, I poured myself into my own cab and asked the driver to take me to a decent hotel somewhere. The meal had been expensive and the hotel twice the cost of that, but Roy, who signed my expenses, knew how much business those guys brought in and what was involved when entertaining them.

The first time I stopped away for the company I'd been told off for staying somewhere that was far too cheap. "It shows the other area managers in a bad light," Roy said. "They're all staying in much more expensive places than that." I didn't want to face the wrath of my colleagues, so from then on, knowing the ground rules, I adopted a different attitude. If there was a five-star hotel in town, that was where I stayed, and in the evening I ate in their expensive restaurant. None of my expenses were ever questioned, including the brandy fest with the Cally Boys. "You've worked hard. Go enjoy yourself and spend some money" was a mantra I heard from Roy more than once. As a good employee I followed orders and did my best to comply.

With Sarah now long departed, I started dating another girl, Frances. Happily, they were complete opposites. Frances had a sunny disposition, was kind, caring, and loving. We married, moved out of my flat and down to the West Country. Edison Halo had sacked their man who covered Devon, Cornwall, Avon, Wales, and Gloucestershire. He'd been running his company car as a taxi – a clever, if unethical idea, as all costs were being covered by the company at the same time as he was drawing his monthly salary. I'd long wanted to move to the countryside, and this was too good a chance to pass up. I asked Roy if I could go and sort out the mess down there. The London patch was running smoothly and would be easy for a replacement to manage. Roy readily agreed to the move, and we were off.

Fran and I did a bit of hunting around and eventually found a brand-new house just outside the small market town of Dursley, in Gloucestershire. It backed onto farmland and was splendidly rural by my standards, but within easy distance of the motorway network. I drove hundreds of miles a week, which was a pleasant change from the stop, start, struggle of London traffic, and when I stayed away, it was in the best hotels as I'd been instructed to do. The flat had sold easily and for a sizeable profit. We took on a small mortgage, still had some money in the bank, and enough disposable income to enjoy a decent standard of living. It had been six years from the day I'd driven away from The Kings Road Theatre for the final time. I had finally moved on.

Bob Norton had joined Halo at roughly the same time as me. He was in charge of the Midlands area, and despite being completely different characters in every way, we got on well. On his first week with the company, he came out with me (supposedly to show him the ropes). I was as green as he was, but we muddled through and after that became good mates and teamed up often. Bob was forthright, at times very blunt, and I balanced that out with a more measured, diplomatic approach. Not quite good cop, bad cop, our tag team produced results and great sales figures. Bob was a highly qualified electrician, whilst I could barely wire up a plug, but I bluffed my way through and smoothed ruffled feathers, while he solved any technical issues.

My new patch had a lot of sorting out to do, and we worked long, hard hours to open accounts, bring in new business, sell at exhibitions, and fix all the inherited problems from Mr Taxi. There was one issue around the lighting at a rather splendid five-star hotel in Devon. We resolved it in a day but decided to stretch it out to another two and have what we considered to be a well-deserved luxury break. Nobody queried what we did or the money I spent. I was left alone and judged on results. Today, it's a totally different world, and I doubt I could hack it out there in that working environment. I certainly wouldn't want to try.

Then came some changes at Edison Halo. The managing director who had first interviewed me left in a hurry, and a new MD was installed. I got on fine with them both, but like an uneasy volcano, I could sense something happening under the surface. Roy made a silly move to try and oust the new MD, having been partly responsible for getting rid of the first one. It was a huge error of judgement and resulted inevitably with him being dismissed. I wasn't interested in any of the politics or games that might be being played out at head office, but it was unsettling nonetheless. In those moments I got the inevitable scent of decline, which ultimately was proved to be correct. It was time to move on again.

By coincidence, one of the electrical trade papers had an advert for a salesman/representative in the area I covered. I knew the company had a high profile in the industry and was long established with a reputation for a great quality product. This seemed like an opportunity that might not come around again. I applied, went for the interview with the sales director and his area manager, and was hired that same day. There had been a number of applicants, and when the area manager, John Robinson, rang to give me the good news, he boosted my confidence massively, saying that I had been the outstanding candidate and their decision to employ me over the others had been swift.

Ashley Accessories manufactured the majority of their electrical products at three factory sites in Cumbria, in the north of England. Where Edison Halo were a bit brash, with big offices and somewhat American in their operation, Ashley were solidly northern working class, personified by the managing director Fred Pickles. He was always referred to as Mr Pickles, never Fred. When I met him for the first time, he was exactly as his name suggested. His suit was old-style, in old-fashioned country check material, worn with a highly polished pair of sensible shoes. His office was tiny and unpretentiousness, with a simple wooden desk, chair, a telephone, and some filing cabinets. I'm not sure if Mr P even had a secretary; I doubt he did. He was a bit like an old-fashioned bank manager. The sort of solid northern man whose word was his bond and whom you felt you could trust.

Just after I joined, we had a meeting with the other guys of the outside sales force where I was introduced to George Van Eke, who'd been around the industry for a long time and was approaching retirement in a few years. Shaking my hand he said, "Congratulations. I don't know if you've worked for a good company before, but you're working for one now." I soon discovered George was an able judge.

The area I had responsibility for had been newly created but had previously been covered by two other representatives. One of them was a Welshman called Mike. I spent a couple of days out with Mike, being introduced to what would now be my customers. He had the gift of the gab for sure and an ego to match. He told me repeatedly how wonderful he was at his job, how it would be difficult for anyone (that being me) to follow someone as well liked and respected by everyone as him. By the end of day two I was wondering if I had done the right thing taking this job. The propaganda was seeping into my brain, and I wasn't sleeping, wondering how the hell would I be able to live up to this guy.

Day three, I was out with Don Phillips, who lived in Devon and was gifting me his customers in Bristol and Bath. Don was an elder statesman, laid back with an extremely dry sense of humour. He had a large geographical area to cover, and as retirement beckoned I think he just did enough to keep people happy without going the extra mile. By the end of the day with Don, I was confident that with some closer attention and hard work I could improve on the figures his customers were returning, but I wasn't sure how the hell I was going to improve on Mike's.

For my induction into the company, I travelled up by train to Ulverston in Cumbria, in the Lake District, where I was met by my immediate boss John Robinson. The train was late arriving which wasn't my fault, but I felt guilty anyway. It wasn't an auspicious beginning. The station was small and when the train pulled in, the platform was empty, apart from a little head peeping around the corner at me. It was John. I apologised for being late and explained the reason. John didn't say much in return which wasn't reassuring, but we chatted in his car and drove the short distance to the main factory in Ulverston. I needn't have worried too much. John was a good guy and although we always maintained the formal relationship that work required, we became friends and happily still are.

I toured the Ashley factory with one of the foremen who took me through every department. It was both fascinating and reassuring. The attention to detail, quality, and care that went into producing all the components was fantastic. The workforce were also impressive, with a great attitude. After I'd been with the company a while, I would take visitors on factory visits, and although I didn't have to, I would always go round with them on the tour. The workers answered questions, thanked the visitors and me for the orders that had been placed and for the work we did, aware that their guests helped to keep them in employment.

Whenever I went through the works engineering section, the smell of white water oil (a lubricant used when cutting metals) and the noise of the machinery brought back memories of when I was fifteen and my first job. That was sixteen years before. I could never have imagined back then I would be working as a company representative, wearing a suit and tie to accompany customers around a similar workshop to my own. Had life been different, it could easily have been me on one of those machines, and it's likely I would have been happy with my lot, as they all seemed to be. They had found their niche, and in many ways I was envious of them for it.

I started doing the rounds of my accounts, beginning with those closest to home – the ones that Mike had previously called on. Their reaction was surprising. "Thank goodness" (and stronger adjectives) "he's gone. We don't have to put up with him any more. What an egotistical windbag he is," they said, meaning poor Mike. It explained why when we had visited some branches together, no-one had taken up his offer of lunch, and I'd noticed a few people quickly disappearing when we came through the door. Man, I had been so gullible buying into all his nonsense and worrying if I could rise to the challenge. Now I felt sorry for him. I never thought him a bad guy, just a very insecure one. That knowledge, though, was a comfort and made my life much easier. I knew I could improve on what had gone before.

As well as maintaining Ashley's existing customer base, we managed to persuade more local authorities to include the company's products on their specifications. And during a housing boom a number of big electrical contractors who were doing a lot of work were persuaded to switch their existing products to ours.

Factory visits were a good tool to promote the company, and I would do my best to persuade anyone looking for quality reassurance to come on one of those. I did quite a few even though I found them exhausting. First, I'd pick up three people from either Bristol, Wiltshire, or Gloucestershire. Then it was a long drive to our first scheduled stop – lunch at the Tickled Trout Hotel and Restaurant just off the M6 at Preston. It overlooked the Ribble River and became a favourite of mine on these journeys. After lunch we'd drive to one of the best hotels on the banks of Lake Windermere, do a boat trip across the lake, followed by pre-dinner drinks in the hotel bar. Then after the meal, more drinks in the bar and maybe a game of pool accompanied by more drinks.

There was no question of me going up to my room until the last guest decided they would retire for the night. They could drink as much as they wanted (although I don't remember anyone being too extreme), but I would drink very little, as getting drunk in front of customers would have been a bad look and I had a full day's driving to do the next day. Then it was breakfast at eight and drive down to the factory for the tour. Afterwards we would meet with the Marketing Director, Managing Director, or sometimes both. There was no hard sell at any point and no pressure on anyone throughout the time we spent together.

With business done, I'd drive our guests to lunch about forty minutes up the road to another restaurant I enjoyed, run by a forthright Irish lady. She'd work the tables throughout the meal and chastise any diners who didn't eat all their food, especially vegetables. Her theatrical performance was one of the reasons I went there, and it always made me smile. Fifteen minutes after leaving the restaurant, we would be on the M6 motorway, and five minutes after that I could guarantee my passengers would all be contentedly fast asleep, leaving me to concentrate on the long drive back, accompanied only by the sounds of light snoring. I'd finally arrive home late after dropping everyone off and be pretty worn out. Okay, I admit it wasn't as hard as digging ditches for a living. I was eating in fine restaurants and staying in excellent hotels with everything paid for, but a five-hundred-mile round trip and two days of entertaining customers was nonetheless always tiring.

Both sets of our parents now lived a distance away. Although Fran and I visited frequently, we spoke about trying to move everyone closer, into what we knew was a better quality of life. It wouldn't prove difficult to persuade my parents to move to the country. They'd lived in the same council house all their married life, and my mum had harboured an ambition to own a bungalow for all of that time. Dad loved the countryside, and on the frequent occasions they stayed with us he hated the thought of going back to what he described as the madness of life back "there". That's not something you want to hear. Then, being burgled and feeling unsafe afterwards helped to cement my idea of getting them out of "there".

For those who are unaware, the Thatcher government of the 1980s decided to sell off the country's stock of social housing. For my parents, it was too good a deal to turn down. Taking into account the number of years they had lived in that house, it was ludicrously cheap, and despite my socialist principles I didn't blame them a jot for taking it. We loaned them a small amount of money to help the purchase, and stage one of the plan to move was in place.

At the same time, I started looking for a large house; one that would accommodate two families. A bungalow wasn't on the list – that was for my parents – but this house would be jointly for Frances, me, and her parents. The plan was for me to continue working with Ashley but for the rest of the family to set up and run a bed and breakfast business. We looked at a number of houses, none of which ticked all the boxes, bar one, just outside of Tetbury. It was a fantastic property but a few thousand pounds beyond financial reach. The location of "Royal" Tetbury, with Prince Charles and Princess Diana's house just up the road, would have been a huge draw for business but pushed the purchase price up as well. It was just too much of a stretch.

On the other side of the River Severn from Dursley is the Forest of Dean, considered to be the poor relation to the rest of the county of Gloucestershire. Foresters are fiercely independent, with their own unique dialect and history. The Forest sits island-like, bordered by the rivers Wye on one side and Severn on the other, adding to its isolationist feel and culture. Its indigenous population are renowned for not moving away from their beloved forest and are the butt of many jokes as a result. I liked them a lot and was envious of the comfort and contentment of their lives.

In medieval times the Forest was a royal hunting ground and a source of timber for the navy's Tudor warships. Sir Frances Drake reputedly visited many times to choose the best oak timbers which were transported through the Forest and down to the river at Gatcombe. Drake's House is still there and lived in by a couple who we came to know. A quarter of a mile from Gatcombe was a property for sale. I went to have a look. The house was sizeable, with potential for six bedrooms and four bathrooms. It had a large farmhouse kitchen, three reception rooms, a conservatory, and a decent-sized dry cellar. Outside was a huge greenhouse, a six-acre field, two orchards, a large garden, and some outbuildings, including a stable which had a horse in it. There was a lot of TLC required, and I guessed a survey might throw up some issues given the property's age. But it was a lot of property for the asking price, and had it been in the Cotswolds would have been triple that amount. We all visited and agreed we could make it work, with enough space to ensure independence and privacy for all. As expected, the survey pointed out what needed doing, which we costed, and having easily sold our respective properties, we paid up and moved in.

The long job of redecorating and renovating began. I took my holidays to do as much as possible, and evenings and weekends were full of banging, scraping and painting. I did some electrical work which would never have passed proper inspection. Once I'd finished, the number of cables running in all directions in one of the loft spaces looked like an explosion in a spaghetti factory. The draughty windows were replaced, and mains gas was run up to the house to replace the old solid fuel boiler which we could never get to generate enough heat to sufficiently warm the house's twenty radiators. Instead, we installed an industrial-sized gas boiler which did that job perfectly, and the old house breathed life again. To keep all that heat inside, I insulated the three lofts, one of which had a massive wasps' nest over in the corner. I was reasonably sure it was dormant, but the closer I got towards it the more I questioned my judgement and courage to finish the job.

The main structure of the house was in two parts. The original farmhouse at the back had walls so thick they would have withstood a nuclear blast. A much newer addition, but equally well constructed, was the Georgian frontage, complete with an attractive veranda running the whole length of the building. The supporting metal struts were stamped as 1837, giving a probable indication of when it had been constructed. Under the old oak floorboards in one of the front rooms was a water well, which I guess had at one time been the front yard of the farmhouse, but no hidden treasures were discovered anywhere, which was a disappointment. On the positive side, not too many disasters were uncovered either.

The rot was replaced, the remaining timbers sprayed, chimneys, roof tiles, and battens fixed, and everything made as watertight as very old houses allow. Outside, the orchards hadn't been touched for years and were full of brambles, but luckily I discovered an old rotavator in one of the outbuildings, and miraculously it worked. It took weeks to turn over all the ground and get out the brambles before levelling off and sowing grass seed. The fruit trees were mostly in a good state and provided a huge amount of fruit to make jams, jelly, and pies. The rest of the apples, including windfalls, we gave away to old Bill who lived not far away and made potent homemade cider in his cellar.

Once all the major work had been done, we had a pagan-like celebratory bonfire in the field. Up in black smoke went our building rubbish along with items the previous owners had left behind that weren't fit to be given away. It had taken a good while and a lot of hard work, but finally the bed and breakfast opened for business and was highly successful, making a substantial profit. I had little to do with any of that, apart from being the night porter on occasions, as I was accustomed to late nights and didn't have to get up and prepare breakfast in the morning. That was my father-in-law's job. He enjoyed cooking and his English breakfasts became legendary, with guests constantly remarking on the quality and quantity he served up. His other passion was gardening, which was fortunate because it wasn't mine, and he made a magnificent job of that as well. My gardening contribution was to cut the grass, and with three large lawns that took approximately three hours from start to finish.

# CHAPTER 13

I came home to find my drum kit set up in the yard out at the back of the house. The drums had been stored above one of the garages, and for some unknown reason Fran and my mother-in-law thought they would get them out and try to assemble the kit. Unsurprisingly, nothing was where it was supposed to be, and I spent ten minutes putting that right, then took a pair of sticks to play around a little. I hadn't picked up a drumstick for a decade-and-a-half and went to do things that had once been automatic but soon discovered they weren't there any more. Little drum licks that I'd played hundreds of times didn't happen. Over years I'd spent thousands of hours practising this stuff and now it was gone.

I wondered if I'd been a bit too ambitious with my first attempt. Perhaps if I toned it down and tried a couple of simple rock drumming patterns that would be easier. They worked in a fashion, but without the feel and ease I believed I'd once possessed. My attempt didn't last long, but rather than pack everything away, it was easier to move the drums into the old stable block where the horse had once been, thinking I might have another go sometime.

Meanwhile I began looking for a bungalow that would suit my mum and dad. And it didn't take long. One of the local agents had an empty property for sale in Saint Braivels – a small, picturesque village with its own castle, pub, church, and shop, about ten miles away from where we lived. I went on my own for the viewing and thought the house was okay but wasn't quite right and not worth getting Mum and Dad down from London to view. I drove away from the property, and out of curiosity went up a small side road in St Braivels – one I had never driven up before. There were about a dozen houses in total, and halfway up on the right-hand side was a for sale sign outside a bungalow.

It looked promising from the kerbside, so I contacted the agent and got a viewing with the owners the same day. The view from the kitchen and lounge, with its huge picture window, was stunning. That view alone would have sold it to anyone, and it sure did it for me. The house was within easy walking distance of the village and positioned high up, approximately eight hundred feet above sea level, with the Wye Valley far below. You could see the river snaking its way through the vivid green hills towards Monmouth and on further into Wales. I rang my dad and said I thought they should have a look at it before anyone else snapped it up. "We'll be down tomorrow," he said.

I had long settled into the idea that my musical life was finished, but with the drum kit now in the old stable and out of antisocial hearing range, I went out to reunite myself with the past. After mucking around and getting frustrated for a good while, a bit of a spark returned; a memory that I had once been able to do this. Most of the technique I'd possessed was gone, but I knew how I'd got there, and retraced my steps back to the beginning. A slang word musicians use for technique is "chops", and my chops would never be as good as they once were. However, in my time away I had learned other things such as "less is more". It's a cliché, but an accurate one. Listening back to recordings I had made, all I could hear were the mistakes, and although it was too late to rectify those I thought it a good lesson for the future. If there was to be a drumming future.

My visits to the stable were becoming more frequent, and suddenly I found the frustration of not getting it right was becoming less frequent. I was getting somewhere and enjoying playing drums again. To make it more interesting, I installed an old DJ's turntable with a couple of speakers and brought some second-hand albums from a local charity shop to play along with; something I'd done as a kid when I was learning. I had the occasional visitor come to see me out there. Mice, who looked down quizzically from on top of the wall separating the stable from what later became the chicken shed. Then a squirrel popped in one day via the roof of a different shed next door, and once a very large black rat climbed up the stable wall, stopped no more than four feet away and looked me disdainfully in the eye before slowly moving on again. The rat made me feel uncomfortable. It was our long-held eye contact, I think.

Maybe it had been a music critic in a former life and was telling me something. Undeterred, I carried on and was relieved ratty never returned.

I thought it a good idea to tart up the stable a bit to keep the damp and wildlife out. I got a builder to float in a concrete floor with a damp course membrane, and then lay breeze blocks all the way around the walls. I put down an old carpet from the house, made up some simple wooden frames, and cut Perspex for the two windows. All of this kept it warmer, the weather out, and even more of the noise in. I couldn't bring myself to change the stable door and employed the old curtain-across-the-door trick to stop the draught. It didn't work well at all, but for sentimental reasons it made me feel better, like I was retaining a bit of the old stable intact. I hoped the horse would have approved.

There's something hugely fulfilling about being part of a group of people making music. You may not have the greatest voice in the choir or be the best drummer in the world, but you can still be a part of something magical, and when it works it's a kind of drug that makes you want to repeat the experience over and over again.

Drums are not a solo instrument. The drummer's main function is to accompany other musicians, and it's in that context they operate at their best; as part of the rhythm section of a band, orchestra, or whatever configuration you choose. I could continue playing on my own, but now I wanted to see if I could rekindle the feeling of musical interaction that had once been such an all-consuming part of my life.

I knew nothing about the local music scene nor how to get into it. There were no social media outlets back then, so I did the old-fashioned thing and put an advert in the *Gloucester Citizen* newspaper under the music section. I think it said "Experienced Drummer looking for other musicians". I got one reply. A singer, guitarist, and songwriter from Gloucester called Robbie Fisher rang and told me that he came with a bass player, Pete Douglas, and that they were looking for a drummer.

Cautiously sounding each other out, we discussed our respective musical influences. From that brief conversation it was evident that none of us were sixteen-year-old kids looking for pop stardom. There seemed to be enough common ground we felt worth pursuing with a rehearsal. I offered to go to Gloucester, but we agreed it was more sensible for them to come out to me. Our first encounter went well enough. Pete was a good bass player, and Robbie had all the right credentials in the singing and guitar playing department. I wasn't blown away with the collective sound we produced, but playing with other people again was enjoyable, and Pete and Rob had a good time too. We agreed to another rehearsal to see how things progressed.

As they went to leave, Robbie handed me a couple of demos he had written and recorded at home on his Fostex machine – a simple four-track recording device which with some operating knowledge could produce good quality recordings for that time. Back inside the house I made myself a drink and put the demos on the player. I was stunned by the quality of the songs, the playing, and the production. I put them on again and again, and the more I listened the better they sounded. It was a brilliant calling card to give anyone. Here you are, I wrote, performed, and produced this; boom.

A couple of years later the American Bluesman and multiple Grammy Award winner Johnny Winter recorded one of those songs, "Medicine Man". It's a direct lift from the original demo I listened to that night (and still have), only not as well performed. It sounds as though Johnnys version was recorded in a hurry. The tempo wavers, speeds up a bit at the beginning before pulling back again, and the instrumentation isn't completely together at times. The guitar licks, the bass line, vocal delivery, everything is copied from that demo – a huge compliment to the original version and Robbie, who painstakingly crafted it in his tiny, rented attic room in Gloucester.

Rob had suggested the band be called The Survivors. I wasn't bothered much about the name but didn't feel strongly enough to object either. After weeks of rehearsals, our inaugural outing was a Sunday lunchtime session at The Jovial Colliers – a small, well out of the way pub in the Forest, ideal for the first outing of a new project. The gig went off with no problems. I didn't freeze, shake, or feel I wasn't able to do this. The natives were friendly, and we got paid, which is always a good result at any level of the music scene.

The Welsh Harp on the London Road in Gloucester was THE local music venue. The "Harp" was the place for musicians to hang out, have a drink, listen to some music, and network at the same time. Rob was well known there, and as a consequence we began playing The Harp a lot.

The band load-in was off the road and in through the main door, where you walked behind the bar with your gear and into the large room at the back of the pub. The amount of beer that had been spilled on the floor made it feel like walking through treacle. I found the best way was to adopt a Monty Python-style silly walk, picking your knees up, persuading the soles of your shoes to temporarily part ways with the floor until you reached the safety of the carpet in the back room. There was an accompanying noise to go with the sticky walk, which is hard to describe but I'm sure added to the entertainment value of anyone watching. The standard fee at The Harp was thirty pounds per gig, plus a couple of free beers throughout the night. The money wasn't good nor really important; it was just a lot of fun to play, and I seemed to be playing there most weeks.

The Survivors morphed into another band, The Dockery Boys. Pete and Robbie were still onboard, and now we were joined by Derek Rutherford on guitar, Roger Baynam on keyboards and guitar, and Mark Cole on vocals and multiple multifarious instruments. This was my first encounter with Mark, who I still work with today and who is one of the most irrepressible, upbeat, funny, and all-round brilliant guys on the planet. The Docs moved up through the gears, and as audiences grew we began playing at the Gloucester Guildhall and other larger venues in and around the county. It was going well, but like most things in life changes were on the way.

Robbie was a complex character with many demons to overcome. He had talent for sure, in particular as a songwriter, but also had a self-destruct button which he repeatedly pressed when seemingly on the verge of a success. I discovered along the way that he'd exhausted the patience of lots of local musicians and that was one of the reasons he had initially contacted me, having literally run out of drummers prepared to work with him. Some of his behaviour was highly irrational, and despite the efforts of friends who offered help, his suspicion of our motives and his capacity for self-harm meant they came to nothing. It was as though he said, "If you're not careful, Robbie, you're going to succeed here. Better screw it up before it's too late." His publishing deal with Rough Trade, the company who had got his demo to Johnny Winter, dropped him like a stone when he made unfounded accusations against them. At the last moment he cancelled a live appearance on BBC Radio Two's prestigious Paul Jones show, after we had rehearsed in preparation for weeks. He let us know by leaving a message on my answerphone. It said, "This is a message for The Dockery Boys from Robbie Fisher. Get fucked."

It didn't make me angry, just frustrated and sad, even though by then I should have expected it. I admired and liked Rob. He'd helped to get me back into the music scene at a decent level, but there are only so many allowances you can make for a person, and this time we had all had enough.

It was a damp, miserable March night, and I was double parked loading kit back into the car outside The Welsh Harp in Gloucester, when a skinny, ginger-headed guy came over. He introduced himself as Nick, told me how much he had enjoyed the gig, and that he was a bass player. I guess he was networking and putting down a marker should any opportunity arise in the future. Later, when Pete Douglas left The Dockery Boys, Nick Quarmby proved to be the perfect replacement on bass guitar. Nick was an excellent bass player, good guy, and at no extra cost came with a dry as a bone, wicked sense of humour.

Robbie had left The Dockery Boys, and so had Pete Douglas and Roger Baynam. As a result, the Docks reinvented themselves. We moved away from the bluesy elements of the early days, and with the addition of a fiddle player went down a Cajun and Zydeco route which was enjoying a bit of a boom at the time, led by bands like the excellent London-based Balham Alligators.

Christie Arthur played fiddle, mandolin, and guitar. He auditioned with the full band out at my place and was exceptional, picking up everything we played within a minute of hearing it. Mark said to me afterwards, "That little fellers in" – meaning Christie, and indeed he was.

You discover your bandmates' personalities over time, and like all of us Christie had some eccentricities which began to surface after spending time gigging away from home. We played somewhere in Essex, stayed overnight at the promoter's home, and as we were about to leave Christie piped up, "Why is it I never get to drive the van? I want to drive." There was no evidence for the prosecution; nothing we could explain kindly or logically anyway. He was random in many ways, and I strongly suspected this would apply to his driving too, but I hunkered down in the back of the van and closed my eyes (not for the first time in my life), thinking what I couldn't see wouldn't worry me.

We duly set off from the promoter's house with Christie at the wheel, and we'd been going over an hour when I heard Nick shout angrily, "Pull over. I'll drive." I was semi-conscious in the back, dropping in and out of sleep, and had no idea what was going on. It transpired that with Christie at the wheel we'd somehow managed to go in a complete circle, ending up exactly where we'd started an hour and a bit earlier. It was the first and last time he drove the van, but on the way to the next gig he yelled at Nick to pull over urgently. We thought it had to be an emergency. Was he about to throw up, or desperately needed a pee? What was the rush? Nick stopped in a hurry, and Christie jumped out and ran across the grass verge. He wasn't the most athletic person in the world, but we watched in admiration as he impressively climbed over the fence into a field, hugged a tree for a while, retraced his steps, and got back in the van. There was complete silence as we drove away. No-one was quite sure of the appropriate thing to say.

Big Bob booked the music for the Hells Angels bikers rallies all around the country. His girlfriend brought him along to see The Docks playing in Gloucester. Big Bob liked what he heard, and we played a good few gigs for him, including The Bulldog Bash – a large event held just outside Stratford on Avon. The average attendance at The Bulldog Bash was forty thousand people, with bikers turning up from all over the UK and Europe.

It was run by bikers for bikers, with the Angels having an agreement to take care of policing themselves on site. Even with that number of attendees and the potential for confrontation between rivals, I never saw any hint of trouble. As you'd expect, there was a massive number of bikes, lots of chrome, plenty of leather and denim on show, large, sometimes huge guys, who all seemed to be accompanied by a beautiful woman. I guess today the Bull Dog Bash would be considered misogynistic, with the topless bike wash (which I remember being popular), as was the wet T shirt competition held on the main stage with twenty or more contestants at a time. Whatever your view on such things, it was the bikers' event held in exactly the way they wanted it to be.

Set amongst the stands selling food, offering tattoos and bike-related items, was the guy who sold human skulls spread out on an old, dirty white sheet in front of his van. I assumed it was a he, although I never saw the person selling. There was never anyone there trying to pull in custom. There were no prices displayed, no special show offers, buy two skulls and get a free patella bone; nothing like that. I was always curious to know what this person looked like. Was he a grave robber who went out in the middle of the night to replenish his stock, or how did it work? He was at all the shows we played and presumably did enough business to make it worth his while, but my curiosity about his identity never extended to knocking on the van door.

Skull man was also at one of the smaller events in the North where we first met a biker girl called Reanne. She was falling about uncontrollably drunk, rolling around in thick, thick mud, having a thoroughly riotous time. Reanne followed us around for a good while. There was never any "romantic" attachment to anyone in the band, she just enjoyed what we did and liked to hang out with us. She was there when we played Glastonbury Festival, too (on The Acoustic Stage). Mark and I had been backstage after the gig, and as we came out front we saw Reanne talking to Christie. We never found out what he said, but whatever it was she decked him with an impressive swing of her left fist, and he went down like a felled tree. She was quite a gal.

During this time, I was working at Ashley Accessories, but changes were taking place at the top of the company and not for the better. Fred Pickles had retired as Managing Director, and Randal Soley our Sales Director, having moved into that position and done an equally fine job, was also retiring.

The company appointed a new sales director. I was prepared to give him the benefit of the doubt, but it was obvious from the beginning that we were dealing with a different calibre of person and not someone who demonstrated any of the qualities I'd admired in the old regime. John, my immediate boss, had been passed over for the Sales Director's position and felt his best opportunity lay elsewhere away from the company. I stuck it for another couple of months, but it wasn't getting any better so I too handed in my notice.

The new Sales Director rang me at home. "Why are you leaving?" he asked. There was no point in sugaring the pill. "I don't want to work for you," I said. There was a moment's pause while he digested this barb. "Well, who needs you anyway?" was his wounded reply. "So why are you ringing then?" I asked, and the exchange didn't last much longer after that. My predicted outcome for the company's future was ultimately proved to be correct. It gave me no pleasure to be right and was a sad ending to the most stable time in my life.

And so having quit, I found myself back in the land of the professional musician. In my time away the scene had shifted dramatically, and not for the better; most notably there was little to no money any more. I was now playing for the enjoyment and anything I earned was a bonus, but I was back.

Bands split for a variety of reasons. Sometimes there's a dramatic event, like a huge row between one or more members which has been brewing for a while and blows the thing apart. I'm pleased that in the case of The Dockery Boys, it was amicable and by tacit agreement. We knew we'd run our course.

Nick told me he was going to work with a singer-songwriter called Gerry, who lived in Bristol. Mark went off to do some solo stuff. Rich, ever the businessman, concentrated on his profitable guitar teaching school. Derek, as a published author, concentrated more on his writing, which left just me at a loose end. But there were still a few bands out there who needed a drummer, and to keep my hand in and earn a crust I did some deputising (dep) work for those.

Then I got a call from Nick to say Gerry, the singer-songwriter he'd been working with, would like to meet up to see if adding drums to the duo would work. My expectations weren't high. I wasn't sure if a trio was something that would suit me, but because I knew Nick we fixed a date to see what, if anything, worked. We met up at my place and, despite my reservations, the songs were good. More than that, very good in most cases. Gerry played a nylon strung acoustic guitar, not brilliantly by his own admission, but well enough to do the job and hold the thing together. The drums did make a difference, and we were able to thicken up the sound with three-part harmonies which fell into place nicely. After running through about a dozen or so songs, I knew it wouldn't take us long to work up a couple of sets. We metaphorically shook hands on a deal, and I was in.

What I wasn't aware of at rehearsal was Gerry's on-stage persona, which can best be described as manic. He has a sharp brain, sharper wit, and a fearsome determination to make the gig work at any cost. He told me if that meant taking all his clothes off and running around the room naked, he would. I believed him, and although it never quite came to that, I learned to expect the unexpected and was still caught out many times. Gerry always gave one hundred per cent to every gig, but that strength was at times his greatest weakness. Had he been able to back off by as little as five per cent, it would have been even better. Occasionally the five per cent won out and Gerry would make an ill-judged, spontaneous remark which made me squirm on stage and worked against himself and us.

I wanted to grab him afterwards and say, "For Christ's sake, Gerry, can't you just tone it down?" But he would counter with, "I have no control over what comes out of my mouth." And eventually I came to believe he might almost be telling the truth. It was as though he was compelled to push the boundaries, to shock by saying something outrageous. When it was measured properly and worked (as it did on the majority of occasions), it was hugely entertaining, at times bordering on genius.

Gerry and Nick had been working the duo under their surnames as ColvinQuarmby. Once again I was in an outfit with a weird band name, but Colvin Quarmby Fitzgibbon would have made it worse, so we left it, and CQ was the often-used catchier abbreviation.

Thanks to Nick's friendship with the well-known folk musician Phil Beer, we got some gigs on the folk circuit, although we were no-one's idea of a folk band. The first of those was at a festival down in Dorset, where we had to play four gigs in three days. There wasn't much money and no accommodation included, but Nick suggested we borrow his brother's tent and camp on site. I'd never been camping and didn't see myself as a happy camper, but I agreed in the spirit of brotherhood and as a band bonding exercise. On the way to the festival, we stopped and picked up the tent which had been stored in a shed at Nick's brothers house and hadn't seen the light of day for many years. It had been wet when stored away, judging by the smell which became apparent as tent and smell slowly emerged from the shed. But no matter, we were committed to the idea, and after erecting it at the campsite, hoped the fresh air would get rid of its pungent aroma. Then it was show time, and we had dates to play at two pubs in the town.

Getting around town close enough to unload a drum kit wasn't easy. Roads were closed off and security had to be found to open up and access the venues. We made it eventually, and somewhat against the odds – thanks mostly to the force of Gerry's personality – the gigs went well. I can't say they were massively enjoyable, and it crossed my mind a couple of times that I might have made a mistake in agreeing to do this. Playing original songs, some of which required listening closely to the lyrics, in a rowdy pub full of pissed-up punters wasn't my ideal, but we survived and in a small way triumphed in adversity. After the second late night gig, we relaxed with a few drinks before going back to the campsite, which was now in pitch blackness.

Everyone else on site appeared to be asleep, and we hadn't thought to bring a torch. We couldn't see a darn thing and had only a rough idea where our tent might be. With the aid of Nick's Zippo lighter, we stumbled around for a bit, doing our best to dodge guy ropes and bumping into other tents, then suddenly

Gerry said, "Hold on, I think I can smell it." And like a bloodhound on the scent, we followed his nose until we could smell it, too.

The following morning I woke up in my sleeping bag feeling a bit cold around the ears. The campsite was slowly waking up, too, and the smell of bacon frying worked its way into my nostrils, which was way more pleasant than the tent's continued aroma. Something else we non-camping types hadn't thought to bring was food. Between the three of us, we had two apples, a banana, and nothing to drink.

The next two gigs went well. The first of those was in another pub, with its usual chaotic entrance. I had to make several journeys and fight my way in through already well-oiled patrons, using my drum cases as a battering ram to force a pathway through to the playing area. "Scuse me, sorry, coming through, mind yer backs" and so on, with each trip.

Our final effort of the weekend was in the main theatre, a kind of civilised reward for the previous tougher gigs we'd worked our way through. The reception we got at the Theatre was outstanding and proof that in the right environment what the band was doing was going to work. We didn't yet have anything to sell, but at the end of the evening went out to the merchandise area in case there was someone who might want to chat or show some form of interest in the band. There was a queue of people waiting who mainly wanted to speak to Gerry, which was completely understandable and something he was extremely good at, whilst in those situations I've always felt like a spare part. I'd be hanging around on the periphery, not really knowing what to say to strangers' compliments other than thank you, but doing my best to support the team effort.

Next up, Nick was due to go on tour with The Phil Beer Band, and Phil very generously suggested that CQ play support on that series of dates. It wasn't a massive tour, perhaps ten or twelve gigs at most, and there was no money on offer, but we grabbed the idea willingly and I'm delighted we did. It was a lot of fun. We would open the evening with a stripped-down, thirty-five-minute set before Phil and his full band did their stuff. We slept on very kind people's floors, and if we were lucky they had an airbed or a welcome sofa to curl up on.

Nick travelled with the other guys in their band van, while Gerry and I went around in his small Ford KA car. Gerry drove in the way I would have expected, which reflected his manic stage persona, those dents and scratches on the car bearing testament to some debatable driving skills. We did a decent amount of mileage every day, had a lot of laughs, and fortunately didn't hit anything. There were no pre-planned stops enroute, but we managed to find plenty of fascinating places, nonetheless. Churches, nearly all of whom had a story to tell, the occasional seaside town, and naturally enough a good number of pubs. Those gigs did CQ a lot of favours, introducing us to enthusiastic audiences and promoters alike. Later, we went back to play those venues in our own right, this time earning a modest amount of money and spreading the word that this was an entertaining band worth seeing.

Things moved quickly after that. We began playing more and bigger festivals. The names we shared those stages with got bigger too, and the response was amazing at all of the venues we played. Having got ourselves a solid base and with more money coming in, we felt it time to beef up the sound with an additional guitarist. Johnny Harris is a talented guy, with a variety of skills as a writer, technician, and musician. John came on board and did a great job, but because of other commitments he was unable to make all the dates. We were recommended another fine player, Dave Dutfield, who subsequently shared gigs with Johnny. When John wasn't available Dave filled in, but running two guitarists didn't make life easy, nor was that arrangement going to be workable long term. Learning new material had to be done twice and drew inevitable comparisons between two slightly different interpretations of the same song. Johnny was involved in other projects and unable to commit full time, whilst Dave was free and keen to take any dates he was offered. They were both excellent players, but a choice had to be made.

Fairport Convention owned Woodworm Recording Studios in Barford St Michael, Oxfordshire, and they had very generously allowed us (at no charge) to rehearse in the studio with Dave Dutfield on guitar. Fairport run their own festival at Cropredy – a small, peaceful, Oxfordshire village transformed once a year by an influx of twenty thousand or so festival-goers – and CQ had been booked to play there. Johnny was in the CQ driving seat and under the impression he was going to play the gig. A conversation was had, and a difficult decision reached. John had cut short his holiday in order to play at Cropredy, and Gerry drove down to tell him Dave was going to be on guitar from now on. To his credit, Gerry had the guts and the decency to do it face-to-face, rather than by phone. It can't have been pleasant, and I learned afterwards that John didn't take it well.

The exposure Cropredy gave the band was a massive help and opened up opportunities to appear at more major festivals. We played all of the largest and best of the day – Shrewsbury, Warwick, Trowbridge, and many others – plus picking up plenty of art centres, folk clubs, and independently run venues, too. By now we had an excellent following, a large mailing list, and were selling out just about everywhere we went.

Gerry had a bad habit (he had a few, but in truth, don't we all?) of making announcements from the stage inviting people to meet up after the show. At The MAC Theatre in Birmingham he randomly said, "I tell you what, let's all go for a curry afterwards." It was a typical Gerry throwaway remark meant in jest, but when we finally got outside the theatre we were amazed to find forty or more people waiting patiently to go eat with us. Luckily Birmingham has enough late-night Indian restaurants to choose from and the owners were delighted when forty-plus people turned up all wanting to spend money. In fairness, it was a cracking night.

Gerry would sometimes ask from the stage if anyone would like to put us up for the night. Strangely, that worked as well. Some of the places we stayed were extraordinary and owned by some incredibly lovely, not to say brave people voluntarily agreeing to give four musicians a bed for the night. We had no idea where we might end up. Post-gig at Winchester Arts Centre was a typical example. Having offered their house as refuge, we followed Richard and Estelle – a couple we'd never met previously – back to their place. As ever, we weren't sure what it might be when we arrived. On the journey we would speculate. A three-bedroom semi perhaps? A small country cottage? it didn't really matter; anything was welcome, and it was always generous of people to offer such hospitality. After a short drive, their car stopped in front of a large set of gates which opened electronically, and we swept into the courtyard of a former convent with more rooms to spare than a Holiday Inn.

Along the CQ road we'd got ourselves a willing volunteer manager, Ken Brown. Ken was a big music fan who first saw us at the Gosport and Fareham Folk Festival and quickly became a great friend, as well as doing a top job with all the things we couldn't or preferred not to do. He came with us for the first seven days of our European expedition, starting in Belgium. I'm not sure if the French-speaking natives of Belgium understood or appreciated what we did, but it was fun, and off-stage we had a fine old time, too. One of the gigs was at an old-fashioned Belgian pub, run by friends of friends. We were staying there for a few nights, and after our gig the owners told us they'd decided to go away for a couple of days and asked if we would look after the place for them. They added, in all seriousness, to help ourselves to anything we wanted from behind the bar! It was akin to putting rats in charge of the cheese store.

The tour moved on to Holland, which rapidly became one of our favourite places anywhere to play. We had two gigs to play in Haarlem – a Flemish-style city not far from Amsterdam, in the northwest of The Netherlands. We rolled into town, Gerry, Nick, Dave, Ken, and me, in our old yellow ex-Automobile Association van, with nowhere booked to stay. The first hotel we came to, just on the town's outskirts, looked suitably rundown and therefore – hopefully – inexpensive. Gerry went in to ask the cost and came back with a big grin on his face, saying he'd negotiated a great price. Job done, we checked in, literally threw our bags into the rooms he'd booked, and walked into town to relax and enjoy ourselves.

Haarlem is a very cool place, with significant architecture, laid-back bars, good beer, and friendly local inhabitants, all very typical of Holland and the Dutch people. It helps that seemingly everyone in The Netherlands speaks better English than we do.

I was chatting to a local in one of the bars, trying to discover why this was. Yes, he told me, they were taught English in school and watched some British television programmes which included comedy shows. That alone didn't convince me, nor did it explain how the Dutch understood the irony in British humour, something which the English-speaking Americans largely don't get. Then he floored me by saying, "Yes, it's an oxymoron." I gave up after that and bowed to his superior use of my language.

It was late when we finally returned to the hotel. There was no night porter, but we'd been given a front door key, so we let ourselves in and everywhere was quiet. In the corridor leading to our rooms was a large Hammond organ and somebody (most probably Gerry) decided it was a good idea to have our picture taken, one by one, sitting naked at the organ. With alcohol-loosened inhibitions and no sense of judgment, we each stripped in turn, giggling like kids, took the photos, then settled down for the night. If there's a security camera video out there of five inebriated idiots stripping off in a corridor to photograph themselves, I'd be curious to see it.

Gerry and Nick were in their twin room at the back of the hotel, with me, Ken, and Dave in a triple at the front. Around three am, our room began to vibrate gently, accompanied by a strange rumbling noise. I woke up, my foggy brain wondering if there was an earthquake happening as the noise and vibration grew in intensity. In our haste to find somewhere, none of us had realised the hotel was near the railway station, and about fifteen feet outside of Nick and Gerry's open bedroom room window was the railway track, so close you could almost reach out and touch the trains going past. In our room it was bad enough, but at the back of the hotel Nick and Gerry's beds started to bounce across the room. There were no passenger trains at that time of the morning, but goods trains started operating at three am, and each one of those took minutes to go pass. They were thoughtfully spaced, though, so that you'd just get back to sleep when the next set of noisy, slow-moving wagons rolled on through. Knackered through lack of sleep, Gerry reminded us in the morning over breakfast that it was cheap.

Up to this point I haven't said anything about our guitarist Dave Dutfield, who was from the Rhondda, a former coal mining valley in West Wales. Dave told me about some of the first places he played as a young guitarist. Miners' welfare halls and working men's clubs in tough working-class areas weren't an easy introduction to playing live, but if you could cope with that you could survive in most situations. At Dave's very first gig, some big guy came up to the stage and demanded the band "Play some Elvis". One of the band replied meekly, "We don't know any Elvis", which fell on deaf ears. "Play some Elvis," said Mr Big repeatedly, the same phrase getting louder each time, until the band complied by busking something that kept him happy.

Dave's experience mirrored mine in many ways. You did what you had to do to survive the evening. Some of my very early gigs had been a bit scary, and when testosterone-fuelled fights broke out, which was almost inevitable, your first thought was to protect your equipment and yourself from any harm. I had to bob and weave a couple of times as glasses flew in my direction. It was a more dangerous version of the flying board rubber game, thrown by my teacher years before.

Dave is smart, a lovely guy, and a wonderfully sensitive guitar player. As the band got a following, guitarists would come and stand in front of him just to see how he did it. He gained his own little fan club of followers, and rightly so. What was surprising to me, and would have been to them, was that Dave wasn't at all well-coordinated until the moment you put a guitar in his hand. From there everything flowed effortlessly. At a Country Fair we played in The Netherlands, it took him around three minutes each time to climb a gate going back to the cottage we'd been given to stay in. We stood waiting and watched his limbs failing to coordinate with each other, his efforts not helped by him laughing continuously at his predicament. It was absolutely and completely different any time he picked up a guitar.

On our first trip to Holland, we took Dave up a windmill (he was agoraphobic), down into a submarine (he was claustrophobic), and he coped with them both admirably, although getting him out onto the windmill's balcony took some time and he looked as though he was treading through treacle to get there. When we had the luxury of staying in a hotel, Dave and I always shared a room. He was a good roommate, although he could never figure out how anything worked and was convinced it was broken until I showed him the simple solution. Then he would break into helpless laughter at his own ineptitude. Showers were a particularly puzzling piece of apparatus. He never quite got up to speed with the different options available, or that on some models you had to lift a little widget to transfer the water from bath to shower. Televisions were another mystery. "Mart, I can't switch the TV on. I think it must be broken," he'd nearly always say.

I'd have a quick look, knowing it was likely to be one of two things. "It's not switched on at the wall, Dave." Or, "You have to push that little red button on the remote, top right." Then when it worked, he'd say in his Welsh accent, "Oh yeah. What a twat!" and burst into laughter. He's great. I love him a lot.

It was Dave who introduced me to Geoff Gurd, someone he'd worked with when backing The Flirtations – a girl trio from the USA. "Nothing But A Heartache" was a single of theirs I was aware of, and is a great record. The "Flirts" flew over to the UK for one date, in Wigan, home of Northern Soul – a big dance craze in the 1970s. I was asked to play drums on the gig, along with Dave on guitar and Geoff on keyboards. Geoff handed me a worn-out tape recording of a live gig, with all the songs in the exact order we would play them. There was to be no rehearsal. I had to learn the songs and arrangements from the tape, turn up and do the gig. I hadn't written anything down, but did my homework and successfully remembered what it was I had to play. The place in Wigan was packed, there was no-one else on the bill, and the crowd were all there to see The Flirtations. There was great music that night, fabulous dancing, and a queue formed after the gig to get the girls to autograph copies of their albums before they flew back to the States the following day.

Geoff lived in Switzerland and had mentored a young girl singer called Victoria Hart, who he thought had a real chance of making it in the world of music. Victoria was around eighteen years old and a lovely, unaffected girl with a fine, husky jazz-style voice. Unlike Geoff, I was never convinced that she was going to take the world by storm, but I'm a tough crowd and would have been happy to be proved wrong. Geoff thought it would be a good idea to give Victoria some experience of live work, and Dave Dutts rang me to ask if I would like to come to Switzerland to play a few dates around New Year's Eve. It was too good an offer to refuse. Would I? Yeah, you bet I would.

I flew into Geneva and took a magical train ride past the lake and then up through the mountains. As the train gently wound its way upwards, everywhere looked like the perfect Christmas card, with pristine snow covering those magnificent Alpine peaks. It was the most incredible picturesque train journey imaginable. I got off at Château d'Oex station and Geoff was there to meet me. We climbed into his car and rattled off, literally, with the car's snow chains crunching their way along the icy roads. It was dark when I arrived at the rented apartment I was to stay in. The apartment was very impressive, but it had been a long day, and I thought I'd get some rest ready for the busy times ahead. I got a beer from the already well stocked fridge and turned in for the night.

The following morning when I opened the curtains, it was an extraordinary sight. The view literally made me gasp. The Alps were right there in front of me, intimidating in their sheer size, magnificence, and unbelievable beauty. Not for the first, or last time, I was grateful for the incredible places music had taken me.

Château d'Oex (pronounced Day) was, as my dad might have put it, the poshest place I've ever been. The Hollywood actor David Niven had once lived there, and up the road was Gstaad where royalty, the rich and famous spent their time skiing and partying. This "poshness" came nicely into focus when I met "Uncle Dave" on my first morning in Switzerland, Geoff and I walked back to his equally splendid apartment, only a short distance away from the place I was staying. Geoff and his partner Lyn had a large Bernese dog, and when they were away on business or holidays, they had a dog sitter come and stay – Uncle Dave. When we arrived at Geoff's apartment, he was sitting in front of the picture window, with the Alps a stunning backdrop, a roaring log fire on one side of him, and a mug of tea in his hand.

"Allo, mate," he said in a London accent I knew so well. "Ow are yer?" He wasn't anyone's blood relative. Geoff had nicknamed him Uncle Dave after the sitcom television character Uncle Albert, from "Only Fools and Horses". They looked alike with their white beards, and they spoke in exactly the same way. What made it brilliant was that when he wasn't dog sitting in this "posh" part of the world, Uncle Dave lived in a small caravan in the corner of a field in Bishops Stortford, Hertfordshire. The irony of that always made me smile. That he was able to enjoy a totally different lifestyle for a high percentage of the year.

We ended up spending a good amount of time together, and he was one of those people who'd strike up a conversation with anyone. It was difficult to leave anywhere without Uncle Dave stopping at a table to say to some bemused person, "Allo, mate, cor that pie looks luvvery," or something like that. If you stood still anywhere long enough, he would be chatting away with one or more of the people around you. He was totally endearing, a real character, and I enjoyed his company immensely.

Uncle Dave came to a festival CQ played, where Osibisa – a well-known seventies Afro Rock band – were on the same bill. Typically, he went over to them backstage. "Allo, boys," he said. "I saw you play at the Roundhouse in 1975. You was bloody brilliant." And the Osibisa boys chatted away with him for the next twenty minutes or so.

My favourite Uncle Dave story was when he got stuck in the lift at Geoff and Lyn's apartment. He was coming back from walking the dog, got in the lift, and halfway between floors it suddenly stopped. There was an emergency button to press, and a female voice answered speaking in a language Dave didn't understand. He dealt with it in his usual manner and in a typically English way. "Allo, mate," he said. "Uncle Dave here. Stucko in lifto."

A few years down the line the old boy passed away in Bishops Stortford, and Geoff organised a whip round to pay for his funeral. He may have been penniless at the end of his life, but whilst in Switzerland he lived like a king.

Geoff decided to make an album with Victoria in the UK, and I suggested a studio called FFG in Bredon, Gloucestershire, somewhere I'd recorded many times. A deal was struck with the studio owner, and to rehearse for the upcoming recording I stayed at Dave Dutfield's house in Wapping (London) for a week. Dutters drove us to a rehearsal studio situated at the back of a music store, and we worked for six or seven hours a day on the tracks to be recorded. After that we decamped to Bredon and FFG. Geoff and Lyn had rented a large house for us all around a fifteen-minute drive from the studio. It was summertime, the weather was good, and the house was comfortable with extensive, well-tended gardens, including a lake you could go punting around if you were so inclined. We drove daily to the studio, worked solidly throughout the day, and relaxed by eating out at a different place each evening. It was a fun, good time experience.

I'm not sure how much of what follows is the truth, or just record company and media hype. Knowing a little about how these things work, my money's on the latter. Victoria, who had sung at the Cannes Film Festival, was still looking for the right break by working as a singing waitress at the Naked Turtle restaurant in London. From there, the story goes, she was invited to perform at a benefit party on George Clooney's yacht. It sounded like a piece of newspaper and record company collusion. Cooking up a good story of a poor little waitress being whisked out of poverty in a modern-day rags-to-riches story. But it worked, and Victoria made all the tabloids on the same day, fuelling my suspicions of collusion. As a result of Mr Clooney's gig, Victoria signed a record contract with Decca Records reputably worth a million dollars – something which I imagine was a vastly exaggerated figure, but I'm cynical about most things connected to record companies and newspaper journalism.

The album recorded at FFG was released by Decca the same year, 2007. The last time we spoke, Victoria was relaxing in a hammock on a tropical beach somewhere, enjoying the moment. Despite her exotic surroundings and all the attention of the moment, she seemed as grounded and unaffected as ever, which pleased me most of all.

Victoria released a couple singles via Decca, including one track we had recorded at FFG, but her singing career didn't work out, and the last I heard she was a show girl dancer working in Las Vegas.

Manager Ken's seven-day stint with us in Holland was coming to an end, but not before we played at Wateringse Folk Stichting, where Hans, the tall Dutch organiser, was delighted with how things went. So delighted he kept repeating "it was fucking great" every few minutes to show how pleased he was.

We saw Ken off at the station in a scene reminiscent of *Brief Encounter*, without the same degree of romance. We stood on the platform and watched the train pull away. It was sad to see him go.

These days Ken promotes gigs, very successfully, down on the south coast and is still a great friend. He's also the owner of the Naked Organ photographs and keeps them in a safe place as a kind of Mafia insurance policy.

On the four of us went, playing a number of Irish bars which weren't at all appropriate for a band like us, but the good-natured Dutch responded well and we got away with it. There were memorable and contemplative moments at Arnhem – the scene of a poignant World War Two operation – and some peacetime madness at Erik and Joke's farm, which defies description on here or anywhere else. You would have to go and see for yourselves, which is possible as they run the only Farm and Country Fair in The Netherlands, at Aalten. You can say I sent you.

After Ken's departure, the amount of sleep didn't improve very much. We stayed up far too late, drank too much, ate rubbish food, and laughed most of the time. In comparison to the UK, we'd gone backwards with accommodation and gig fees, but it was an expedition of discovery and, above all else, enjoyment.

We went back many times to The Netherlands after that first trip, and my memory of the chronological order of events and visits has become blurred through time. We established a routine on those European adventures. We'd drive to Harwich and pick up the Catamaran, which was a three-hour bumpy ride to the Hook of Holland. Whatever the weather and sea conditions, it was always bumpy, even on a flat calm day. And on a rough crossing, it could be mighty uncomfortable – for me anyway, not being the best of sailors. Maybe that's why it no longer runs on that route. We would always go straight to the bar and hang out there for the duration. When the bar suddenly closed and the staff began to lock the bottles down and put glasses away in racks, you knew something was brewing up ahead. I have a vision of Dave Dutts hanging onto a bar rail with one hand, trying to eat his favourite apple pie with the other, and laughing at his own failing attempts to connect pie to mouth as the floor beneath his feet bucked around like a Disney ride.

We played a small bar in Amsterdam and did the tourist thing after the gig, walking around the red-light district, only to end up in another bar where the price of beer was outrageous. When we queried the cost, the lady serving shrugged her shoulders and said, "What do you expect in Amsterdam at four o'clock in the morning?" It was a good point, succinctly made, and no-one fancied arguing with the couple of heavy guys over in the corner who seemed to have suddenly become interested in our conversation.

The CQ bandwagon rolled on through the Netherlands. We'd stayed at a promoter's house, sleeping like little sardines, side by side on the lounge floor. The next morning he had to go to work, so we shifted ourselves out uncomfortably early and went in search of breakfast. After a short drive we found ourselves in a docklands area which had seen more prosperous times. It was around nine am by then; the majority of the shops on the main street were boarded up, apart from a couple, one of which was a bar. It was open, and in we went. We weren't alone; there were at least four other people inside, which we thought encouraging and a good sign for a potential breakfast destination. One of those customers sat on the far side of the room to me and was rocking backwards and forwards in his chair, which I took to be a sad affliction of some kind. We sat down at a table and a big guy (not unusual in the Netherlands) came over to serve us.

Gerry said, "Oh, hello," in a cheerful English voice. "We're pleased you're open." The big guy nodded, didn't smile, and said in a gruff voice, "What do you want to drink?" I said, "Can I have a coffee please?" and Dave joined in, "I'll have one of those as well."

"We don't serve coffee," was the curt reply. Gerry had a go. "I'll have a dry white wine then," he said. "We don't have wine.

This is pub. You drink beer." It seemed a bit early, but as there was nothing else on offer, we settled for the beer. All this time I could see the poor guy down the end of bar rocking back and forth in his chair. I didn't want to stare, as it was impolite. Then suddenly, to my amazement, he stood up. What I had taken to be some kind of illness was him working up enough momentum to get to his feet. He staggered, literally, on drunken legs across the room, out of the door, and we watched him weave his way past the bar's plate glass window and down the street. He was gone no longer than five minutes and came staggering back the same way, perhaps figuring he hadn't yet had his full quota for the day, and fell into the chair he'd recently vacated.

In the meantime our beers had arrived, and we discovered we were in the only bar in Holland that didn't serve food of any kind. No matter. It turned out the bar owner's name was Martin, and despite his blunt manner he was a good bloke, which being Dutch doesn't surprise me. We left him a cd, and a couple of weeks later he contacted us to say he much he enjoyed it and was playing it often in the bar. Welcome though that place was, in all conscience I couldn't recommend his establishment as a place for breakfast.

Back in the UK, I'd discovered a percussion instrument called an Udu. Its origin is thought to be Nigerian. The Igbo people are a tribe in southern Nigeria, and in their language Udu means pot, which describes an Udu perfectly. It's a clay vessel; a pot or vase with an extra hole on its side. When you cover the hole, the air is pushed through the pot, out of the neck, and this makes the percussive sound. The technical term for this type of instrument is a plosive aerophone, which is why I always called it a pot. After some research, I discovered a shop in Brighton that sold Udus. So Nick, Ken Brown and I decided to have a day out and take a trip down to see what they had to offer. I bought a large, vivid red clay pot that was rather beautiful in its own simplistic way. On the journey home we discussed a potential song in the CQ armoury that might be Udu perfect, and the following day we travelled to Overstrand, Norfolk, just up the coast from Cromer, for a week's rehearsal at a friend's house. It was an opportunity to try out our idea for the pot.

Like many British seaside towns, Cromer boomed in the Victorian era. The Victorians built a pier – a marvel of engineering which allowed its visitors to walk its one hundred and fifty-one meter arm stretching out into the North Sea. The Victorians knew a thing or two about construction. Cromer pier has withstood storms, tidal surges, and even an attempt to blow it up by the British Government in World War Two to prevent potential use by an invading German force. Almost at the end of the pier is The Pavilion Theatre. I've been lucky to play there a half a dozen times or more, and I love its slightly quirky interior both front and backstage.

Our friends at Overstrand had gone away and left us alone in the house. As was often the case with CQ, we hadn't planned any catering and were saved when another good pal, Fiona, turned up at the house with some breakfast. Fi's dad was a local legend and a crab fisherman. Cromer crab is famous around the world, although not everyone's idea of breakfast. Delicious though it was, man cannot live by crab alone. So, prompted by this kind gift, we did some shopping in town and back at the house got down to some hard work. It was a productive musical week. I thought the Udu might work on one of Gerry's songs called "The Bell", and it did just that. I can't remember the venue for its debut performance, but I'm sure it must have gone well.

The pot quickly became an important part of the show. I had the idea of standing the Udu in full view of the audience, with some flowers sticking out of its neck so that it appeared to be just a prop – a vase of flowers sitting on stage as part of the set. The surprise element came when I removed the flowers, sat down, and laid the pot on its side on my lap. It took a couple of minutes to set this up on stage, but Gerry has never been accused of being lost for words. He would rattle on between songs for minutes at a time, in particular when a train of thought sent him in a direction hitherto unexplored. On a few occasions when he'd been banging on about something for too long, I'd produce a newspaper and pretend to read it. Audiences cottoned on quickly, and their laughter meant Gerry had to turn around to see what was happening behind him. At one venue the whole band managed to sneak off without him being aware, and in another I snuck off backstage, went out an emergency exit, ran around to the front of the building, through the front entrance, and came walking up the centre aisle of the theatre towards him.

Sitting with the large red Udu on my lap, Gerry began referring to it as Mart's giant red testicle. Everyone got the joke, it always raised a laugh, and the song with the pot became a favourite with everyone. When we introduced the vase to Dutch audiences, it was a big hit too and a major help for cd sales. When asked which CD they wanted to buy, the queue of mostly middle-aged ladies always said the one with the big red testicle.

I was on the way from Harwich docks, driving into London to drop Dave at home, when the van's brakes failed. Our old van lived with me, as I had the most room and a secure off-road place to keep it. It had belonged to Phil Beer, and Phil had run it for a good few years before we took it over. The mileometer had broken at one hundred-and-three thousand miles, so we had no way of ever knowing its true figure, but my guess is it was at least double that. There was work to be done on the van, like a new steering rack, but I got a local mechanic to fix whatever was required and it served us faithfully for a long time.

Gerry, who wasn't allowed or insured to drive the van, always insisted he could never travel in the back. He had a kind of claustrophobia that would impel him to lunge forward and grab the wheel, or so he claimed. It seemed more likely that he wanted exclusive use of the more comfortable front seat, but we decided it was prudent not to test this theory just in case. Having the van live with me meant I was the first to leave home, picking up Gerry first in Stratford upon Avon, then Nick in Oxfordshire, before finally we went onto Dave's house in Wapping, London. Everyone got dropped off in reverse order, leaving me to do the red eye run back home to Gloucestershire in the early hours of the morning. Nick was good and drove more than his fair share, with me often stretched out on the back seat, but the final thirty miles on my own could be tough going. I'd try various techniques to keep awake, pinching my ear lobe, slapping myself around the face, and sticking my head out of the window which worked well in winter. When none of that was enough, I'd pull up and have a ten-minute break walking around in the fresh night air.

It was me at the wheel driving into London when the brakes failed. We were coming down a hill towards a roundabout where Dave, who was navigating, had told me to go straight over. I went to slow down, pressed gently on the brake pedal, and nothing happened. I pressed harder until my foot was flat to the floor, but we were still increasing rather than decreasing in speed, heading towards the stationary cars waiting at the roundabout below. I yelled out, "The brakes have gone!" which instantly got everyone's attention, and started going through the gears to try and slow us down with the engine screeching and whining in protest. On our inside was a filter lane for the roundabout traffic turning left. It was on a slight incline, which I quickly decided was the place to go. It was full of cars, but I indicated and started edging my way across to a chorus of horns from angry drivers. The alternative of ploughing into the back of the cars below was worse than their displeasure.

We got over to the slip road just in time, and as I'd hoped the incline slowed us down until eventually we came to a gentle stop. There was a moment's silence while I breathed again and recovered my composure. We'd been lucky and got away, with no damage done to vehicles nor anyone hurt. Then Dave piped up, "We're going the wrong way now. We should have gone straight across at that roundabout." We said in unison, "Dave, the brakes have gone." "I know," said Dave. "But we're still going the wrong way."

# CHAPTER 14

CQ carried on playing our way around the country. In the geographical areas where we were known, it had become easy to fill venues. Anything south of Birmingham felt like our territory and we prospered in it. We ventured north a few times, including a tour of Scotland which was huge fun, but trying to build an audience that far from home was expensive and time consuming.

By now I was booking all the gigs, adding names from the mailing list onto the database, writing newsletters, looking after the merchandise, dealing with the upkeep and maintenance of the van, plus a few other things I might have forgotten. It was my attempt to keep the band out there and to move us forward, but in the process I made some misjudgements and mistakes trying to establish CQ in fresh areas. I'd booked a series of venues at a lower fee than was practicable, thinking once we were established we could make it pay, but it hadn't really worked.

Dave in particular failed to enjoy being in some parts of the country, and the low fee earned was no compensation for his discomfort. I understood his point of view and why he felt that way. In my case it wasn't about the money; it never has been. I've always tried to enjoy the journey and the experience as much as the playing. The camaraderie is important, the memories which only those involved can know about. Phrases, sayings, and shared special moments which years later a single word can recall to those in the know. I love the special places only musical events can take you. That's happened to me multiple times, and I'm sure my bandmates are tired of hearing me remind them every time that occurs, which it does frequently. Places and people you would never get to experience in any other way, had it not been for music. You can't put a price on that. But that's me, and of course not everyone feels the same way. I know there are those who hate the travelling and long hours, miss their loved ones, and would rather be at home tucked up in the embrace of their partner's bosom than loading kit into a van in the cold and pouring rain. I get all that, but when it works, when you've had a great time, feel you've played well, an audience stands to show their appreciation, and everyone leaves with a huge smile on their face, you forget the difficulties of the day, the traffic jam that delayed you by several hours, the bad weather, and all the frustration of whatever you had to do that day to get to this place. In those moments it has nothing to do with money (which is just as well, as there's very little); it's a feeling that for me is priceless and impossible to reproduce in any other way I know. It's going to end one day, and that day is getting ever closer, but I try not to dwell on it.

Sadly Dave had reached a point where he had none of that pleasure or desire any more and wanted out. He would be impossible to replace in many ways and we would miss him hugely, but Nick, Gerry, and I wanted to keep playing, and we had a meeting to find a way forward. Going back to where we started with just the three of us was quickly dismissed. It could work, but we'd become used to having some extra beef in the sound, and the newer songs we'd crafted together worked best with that arrangement. I can't remember who came up with the idea, but there was another suggestion.

Marion Fleetwood played fiddle in a band we knew, and Al Maslen was a guitarist in the same outfit. Both lived in Stratford Upon Avon, the same as Gerry, which we thought might help logistically. And both were good musicians with experience of playing all types of venues. Their own band had almost fizzled out, and although we didn't know Al or Marion well, we thought they might be interested in joining forces. An approach was made and a rehearsal arranged, where it was clear Al and Marion had done their homework in learning the songs. Al tried to replicate a couple of Dave's feature guitar solos, but that was never going to work. Better that Al put his own stamp on those songs, which he did.

We'd never had a fiddle player, so Marion was free to fly her stuff over the top of the arrangements, and that fitted in nicely. Both did backing vocals, and Marion has an excellent singing voice that Gerry chose foolishly never to use. He hadn't done that with me either, even those times when he'd lost his voice, usually through alcohol overindulgence and too many late nights. On those occasions I'd offered to take a couple of the lead vocals – not to try and take the limelight; I could never be a frontman and certainly wasn't going to overshadow a personality as big as Gerry's. But simply to ease the strain from someone who couldn't speak never mind sing. He preferred to croak his way through instead, which I never understood; it sounded awful and wasn't going to help heal the throat. Marion's backing vocals worked well, and having a female voice in the mix added something extra to the sound.

With Marion and Al on board we were up and running again. Our style changed a little, but by an acceptable amount, and still worked well. Al and Gerry had an early falling out when Al quit for a few hours in the middle of a run of gigs, before rethinking his decision and returning. But that's Al for you. Marion is a trooper, who dug in, and despite the teething problems things settled down nicely into lots of excellent dates over a couple of years or more, with everyone doing a great job and getting on well enough.

Whilst I'd been busy on CQ duty, my old Dockery Boys buddy Mark Cole had been indulging in his musical passion of the Blues. Mark had formed a duo with guitarist Rick Edwards, and the pair had been working around the UK and Europe. Mark wanted to have the option of expanding the duo into an occasional four-piece band called Sons of The Delta. Ade Deane was on bass, and I was happy when asked to play drums, even though my knowledge of Delta Blues and Blues drumming in general was, and still is, negligible. Shortly after playing a couple of local gigs in Gloucestershire, we were off to Spain where Mark and Rick had struck up a good relationship with a Spanish agent, Javier Hernandez. Javi had downsized his operation due to ill health, and instead of booking big name artists, now preferred to work with a few select people further down the food chain, like us. Javi had nothing bad to say about any of those major artists, but in some cases they tested his nerve and increased unwanted stress levels.

Van Morrison has a reputation for being awkward, and there are countless stories of how that manifests itself. In fairness to Mr Morrison, Javi's only problem was that he wanted to fly in to play the gig on the same day and then fly home again that night. It wasn't an issue unless an incoming flight was cancelled or delayed. There was one occasion when Javi was at the airport waiting to pick him up from a delayed flight, and the audience were already taking their seats ready for the show. It didn't make for a stress-free promoter's life.

With that in mind, Javi always flew us in the night before the gig, which was fabulous for me as we could relax, have a meal, and spend some real quality time together. The first occasion we went over as a band, Javi picked us up from the airport and drove us back to his impressive offices. Attached to the office was a warehouse full of musical equipment. The guys could have a choice of which amps they wanted to use, and I had three or four drum kits and a host of cymbals for my use. From then on, whenever we went over our choices would be pre-loaded in the van ready for the gig. Most times Javi would meet us at the airport, but on a couple of occasions he sent somebody else in his place.

We flew into Bilbao in the north of Spain, and as we exited customs a young guy came over and introduced himself to us as Luis. He didn't speak much English but managed to convey that the transport was over this way. As we walked across the arrivals hall towards the large doors leading to the concourse, Mark asked him how Javier was. "Is Javi ok?" Mark asked, using what he hoped was the internationally recognised thumbs up sign. Luis looked a bit confused and seemed to be wondering who's Javier? It turned out that Luis was there to pick up another English band and, seeing the guys carrying their guitars had assumed it was us. Javi did pick us up, but he was late arriving that day. Luckily we hadn't gotten as far as driving away from the airport, although I've always been curious what the alternative gig might have been like and what the audience response to us appearing on stage would have been.

Aside from being easy to deal with and cost effective, Javier liked us for another reason. His big American acts only ever wanted to eat at McDonalds or Burger King, whereas we were more than happy to sample the local cuisine, which varied from one region of Spain to another and was mostly delicious. The majority of driving we did in Spain was on motorways, until Javi would suddenly turn off and take a small road into a tiny, often unprepossessing looking village or town. He knew all the best places to go and eat and would ring ahead to make sure there was a table available.

One place I always remember was in a small, sleepy village. We pulled up outside a tiny cafe/bar with two elderly very Spanish looking gentleman sitting outside smoking. I thought it might be okay for a Cortado or a beer, but nothing more. We parked up in the street and followed Javier into an equally rustic looking small bar. I wondered what was going to be so special about this place. Perhaps the tapas was especially good, or maybe we were running late and this was the only available option. Javi carried on through the bar to a pair of double doors at the back and signalled us to follow him. On the other side of those doors was a different world. A large, air-conditioned dining room opened up, with beautiful, starched white tablecloths, smartly dressed waiting staff, and a real atmospheric buzz about the place. The room was full, and we were surrounded by lovely local families all enjoying a delicious meal together in "proper", non-touristy Spain.

That was a lunchtime meal, but if you're going to eat later in the day it's preferable to do that after, rather than before a gig. That way you can relax, knowing the job is done, and it's far more comfortable playing on a waiting stomach than a full one.

After the show we always helped the crew to pack up our gear, and on one particular night by the time we got to the restaurant it seemed a good percentage of the diners had been part of our audience. There was a ripple of applause in recognition as we moved through the room. It was full, but as usual Javier had booked, and we were shown to a spacious reserved table in the centre of the restaurant. People on adjoining tables raised their glasses to us in a toast, and we cheerfully returned their good wishes.

Javi would usually translate the menu, but on this occasion suggested we try a set course meal which included two very special local delicacies, he told us. The starters were a selection of tapas, vegetables in the main, and absolutely delicious. The main course came served on silver platters which the waiters theatrically paraded through the restaurant shoulder-high until two of those large platters landed on our table. One was unmistakably pigs' trotters, and on the other was a Spanish dish called pinna, or pigs' ears. The trotters weren't so much of a shock, but the ears that had once belonged to baby pigs were, and there was no disguising them in their colour and shape. They came coated in an orange sauce and were possibly one of the least appetising things I've ever seen.

It felt as though the whole restaurant was now focusing their eyes on the centre table and us, wondering if the gringos were going to try this dish or not. We felt obliged to uphold our nation's standing and not upset our host's hospitality, so I started on the easy stuff, the pigs' trotters. It wasn't something I would rush to order on a restaurant menu but at least it wasn't an unheard-of dish in my world. I managed a couple, which weren't that bad. I can't say I enjoyed them, but the vegetable accompaniment, washed down with local red wine, was thankfully excellent.

Now came the piglets' ears, and none of us fancied this idea, but the eyes of the restaurant were upon us. I took two and put them on my plate. I can't explain why two; perhaps in my subconscious, ears came in pairs. They didn't appear to have been cooked and were still pink, as if a butcher had loped them off five minutes before. I'd given my dog a few pigs' ears as a treat in the past, and even they had looked a darn site tastier than this. I stared at the pair of ears sitting on my plate. I was reminded of a Tony Hancock film where, as an Englishman abroad, he's presented with a plate of snails and asks innocently, "Does one eat the horns?" I wasn't sure where I was supposed to start. The fleshy lobe seemed as good a place as any, and I cut a bit and put it in my mouth. It was gelatinous, chewy, tasteless and, even with sauce coating, hard to swallow. I didn't gag, but that was enough for me. I thought sod the country's reputation, let the other diners show their derision. I'm not eating any more of that.

Back in the UK and CQ land, Nick became the latest person to quit the fold. We'd had a great run over the years, but Nick later confessed to being "Gerried out", as he put it. Gerry's antics could be wearing, and Nick wanted to pursue his long-held interest in astronomy and planetary science at the Open University. Later, he made a few appearances with the Phil Beer Band, which he'd always enjoyed as a social event with his bandmates. It was also around that time he began to look unwell. I don't know at what stage he knew the prognosis and whether that was part of his decision to leave CQ or not. Nick didn't enjoy a healthy lifestyle. He wouldn't eat regularly and would sometimes go for a couple of days without eating, preferring a pint of beer and a cigarette to anything else on offer.

Gloucester Crematorium was overflowing with people in 2017, including Gerry and Dave Dutfield, of course. Dave and Nick had been particularly close, and Dave was mighty upset, as were many others. It's six years on from his death, and Nick is still spoken about with huge affection. His humour, musicianship, and personality are much missed by everyone who knew him.

For me, CQ was stuttering to an end. Al had gone, and his sometime irrational, selfish behaviour, went with him. Now Nick was no longer involved, Gerry wanted to change things and involve himself in more of the organising role I'd had. That was fine with me. I had only taken on those tasks in the absence of anyone else volunteering their services and in the interest of trying to keep the band out there working. It had been hugely time consuming, and I had never taken a penny piece in commission, so relinquishing that responsibility wasn't difficult. But with that change in dynamic came an attitude shift. The new regime that Gerry wanted to implement was going to be different. "Welcome to my new world" was the phrase he used as he pocketed the CD money after a gig. It wasn't a world that I would be a part of.

It was a messy end. CQ had been a huge amount of fun and opened up a previously unknown musical world for me. Over the years we laughed the majority of the time, created some unforgettable memories, and it was satisfying to help take something from nothing to a small but not insignificant place. Gerry was undoubtedly the major reason for whatever success we had. People came to see him for the excellent performer he was and is, but the show was significantly better due to the other people involved and the role we all played.

The parting shot for me related to the new musical project I had recently started. I said to Gerry that perhaps a clean break between us would be for the best. He told me categorically that what I had planned wasn't going to work. "You'd be better off staying with me," he said. It was a truly insulting remark and a red rag to a stubborn Taurean bull like me. I knew then it was past time to go. There were other interests I wanted to pursue and points to prove that needed to be hammered home.

I'm not sure when I first had the idea of forming my own band. It would have been near the end of my time with CQ and partly borne out of frustration with how the future appeared to be shaping up. I also got tired of hearing my voice asking why a particular band were doing this material and not that. Why another's sets were so one-paced with nothing up tempo to counteract the mournful plod through one depressing song after another. Instead of being critical of others, it was time for me to keep quiet and do something of my own. It wasn't a vanity project. I had no intention of naming the band after me, nor was I silly enough to imagine I could front it in some way; a front man I am definitely not.

Drummers are rarely, if ever, seen as a creative force in any band. Drummer jokes are plentiful and well known. I won't repeat them here. I don't want to perpetuate the myth that we are somehow not proper musicians unable to do anything other than make a noise that resembles someone building a garden shed. Great drummers are as skilled technically as any musician you care to name. Arguably more so in that they have to compartmentalise four limbs to play independently of each other and still have enough head space to sing or deal with whatever else is happening around them. The ability to play drums well doesn't come without a huge amount of dedication and study. In evidence, Your Worship, I offer you the American drummer Mr Vinnie Colaiuta as one such exponent of skill, dexterity, and all-round brilliance. Vinnie is a master of his instrument. Go check him out if you want to see what I mean. The best of the best also play with a touch that doesn't just require great technique but sensitivity (yes, drummers can do sensitivity, too), plus the very hard to define and elusive "feel" that another American, Steve Gadd, so effortlessly demonstrates in his playing. Both Vinnie and Steve occupy the same level of excellence in contrasting ways. Sadly, I can't claim to be in their company, but being "just" a drummer doesn't preclude me from having creative ideas. I have those in abundance, and I wanted to explore my theory of presenting songs that I believed in and which would appeal to many different audiences as well.

I'd been on the folk circuit for years, albeit in a band that wasn't most people's idea of a folk act. To their credit, most audiences listened without prejudice. Folk music was also changing, slowly in some cases, and there would always be a hard core of "folkies" who were purists and tempted to shout Judas, but they were becoming the minority. The present demographic had grown up through the sixties and seventies and their tastes were more eclectic, their minds more open to something different.

I went to see Mark Cole at home to run my thoughts past him. Mark is the perfect bandmate and we've been good buddies for many years. I'm godfather to his two sons, Rory and Josh, and I knew I'd be able to get an open-minded, friendly hearing from him. I explained in detail the kind of musical circuit I'd been playing and why I thought the right band with a slightly different approach would work. I wanted to mix it up, to include a variety of genres that I personally enjoyed and believed others would as well. My intention was to ensure everyone in the band was paid a reasonable sum per gig and would be well looked after. My musical plan was straightforward. I wanted to take a mixture of great songs – upbeat mostly, but with some thoughtful material for balance – and present them in a way that would tug the emotions sharply in both directions. What constitutes a great song is subjective, of course, but as this was to be my project, I insisted on having the final say on what we would and wouldn't play. Every band I'd been in since the age of fifteen had made choices that were never mine and I disagreed with. For the first and only time in my "career", I wanted to try it my way.

Marion Fleetwood played fiddle in CQ, and with her fine voice I thought might be our secret weapon if I could persuade her to get involved. For some inexplicable reason, previous bands had refused to allow Marion to take any lead vocals, as was the case with Gerry in CQ. If Marion was willing, I thought we could give her the platform she deserved and build the band around her. Had she said no, I didn't have a plan B, but luckily she agreed. Rick Edwards and Ade Deane from the "Sons" were the easy choice for lead and bass guitar. We'd worked together many times now, and although neither fully got the concept I proposed, they were prepared to give me the benefit of the doubt and see what might happen.

I found a new rehearsal studio roughly halfway between Stratford, where Marion lived, and Gloucester. It was a splendid old mill in the countryside, well away from any other properties. The young owners were keen to make this proposition work and gave Mark and me a warm welcome when we pitched up for the first time in my car. After showing us around, they disappeared in a haze of distinctive smelling smoke while we unloaded and set up.

It wasn't instantly a blast, as sometimes happens, but it wasn't bad either. Explaining what I was after took some adjustment in their thinking, but there was enough of a spark to gain everyone's interest and a willingness to explore things further the following week. With Mark's help I worked up a method to present ideas in a straightforward way, and over the next few rehearsals the band began shaping up and, dare I say, sounding good.

It wasn't the most pressing item, but I had to come up with a name, and having been in odd-sounding bands it was now down to me to find something I liked. It took a while. I discovered my first choice, The Gigantics, had already been taken by some hip-hop outfit in the States. The closest I could get to that was The Jigantics, which sounded similar, suitably upbeat, and could be shortened to The Jigs, which I liked. It wasn't the greatest band name in the history of great band names, but an improvement on what for me had gone before.

Next on my list was getting some gigs, and I was lucky to have good contacts having booked for CQ in the past. That at least got me a hearing, although it's a crowded market, with lots of hopeful musicians and bands all vying for the limited slots from promoters who need to fill their venues and can't afford to take many chances.

I broke one of my own rules for the first gig. The Bell in Bath describes itself as a bohemian pub and is a well-known music venue with a reputation for putting on excellent bands. Although I agreed a fee for playing, entry was free. In my defence, I wanted somewhere a little out of the headlights but with a discerning, music-loving audience, who I hoped would give us the confirmation I was looking for. I needn't have worried. After song number one, I knew we were going to be fine. The response was excellent, and that continued throughout the whole of the first set. Further confirmation came when I went outside during the interval and overheard a phone conversation with a young couple urging some friends to come down for the second set to hear this band. Then more people came over to say they loved what we were doing. I thanked them, of course, and although I couldn't say it out loud, it did mean a lot. Set two was equally good, as was the all-important atmosphere in the room, and the night ended with smiles all round from audience and band. We knew there were improvements to be made, but for a first outing it couldn't have gone any better.

Before driving off that night I sat alone in the car for a few moments, reflecting on how the evening had gone. Then I metaphorically punched the air. It was a good feeling; a plan that was coming together. Now it was down to me to roll it out and prove the doubters wrong.

I was juggling my time between booking gigs, working on publicity, recording The Jigs' first CD, helping out two other bands with drumming duties, and doing my best to deal with life in general. During this time my dad was being treated for a bad back and spent the majority of the day on the sofa, or in bed at home. I visited every day to see how he was and if he was coping. Mum now had mild dementia, and Dad would be the one doing the majority of the work around the home. Having any kind of condition was just considered an inconvenience, as Dad was someone who didn't make a fuss about anything. Had his leg been hanging off by a thread, he would have said he was fine; nothing to worry about. I'm exactly the same, so I should have read him better and dug a bit deeper. I asked the doctor's surgery to explain what was going on and got a reassurance that the treatment they were providing was the right one and the expectation was for a full recovery soon. Bad backs can be painful and debilitating but there are worse ailments to deal with.

A week later at around two am, the bedside phone rang and I jumped up to answer. It was an ambulance crewman at my parents' house. He came straight to the point. "I'm sorry to tell you, your father has passed away," he said. I hesitated, not knowing what to say. I was now wide awake but struggling to take in this devastating news. I mumbled something. The voice asked if I could come to the house, and I said, "I'll be there in fifteen minutes, but please don't go until I get there."

On the journey I tried to think how this was possible. We'd spoken to the doctor who had been adamant his diagnosis was correct. But no-one dies from a bad back; there had to be something else. When I arrived, the paramedics were as good as their word and had waited for me. I can't remember what was said, but they left soon afterwards while I did my best to console my Mum.

I wasn't sure of the sequence of events and whether she would be able to recall them accurately or not. I thought if that was the case then perhaps it was a good thing, not to relive the undoubted trauma of that night. The ambulance crew had moved Dad into a spare bedroom, and after getting Mum back into her bed and settling her down, I went in to see him. He looked peaceful. The blood had drained from his face, his skin colour was slightly yellow, and his mouth partially open, but there was no visible sign of suffering. I don't think I cried, which is unusual for me as I'm emotional and cry easily; maybe I was still in shock. The biggest influence and support in my life, my irreplaceable best mate wasn't there any more.

The guilt came flooding in. Could I have done more? Surely there was something I'd missed and failed to do. Had I been selfishly too focused on my own life to realise what was happening? I checked again to see if my mother was still ok, then went to the third bedroom and tried unsuccessfully to sleep, listening out for any movement or signs of distress next door, and thought what best to do now for my mum's future. I'd promised my dad that in the event of something happening I would look after her, and he knew I'd do that.

The post-mortem revealed the cause of death was an aneurysm. I was asked if I needed a detailed explanation of what that entailed but said no. I didn't want to relive the event in my head. I hoped it had been swift. The doctor rang, offered his condolences, and apologised. It's likely I would have said there was nothing to apologise for. I didn't apportion blame, and what good would that do anyway? It was all too late.

The Jigantics made good progress on the folk music scene. We weren't anybody's idea of a folk band, which was all part of the cunning plan. There were more than enough artists filling the singer-songwriter and traditional folk music role without needing to add to their number. It made sense to offer audiences something else, a change of diet, and they seemed to love the variety of the menu we offered.

As we were doing so well in the UK, I contacted some venues in Holland to see if we were able to translate that good form into another part of Europe. Three or four theatres where I'd played previously responded well to the idea of us going over the following year. To make the trip viable I needed more gigs and spent most of Christmas, including Christmas Day, researching venues I thought might enjoy what we did and would possibly take a chance on an unknown outfit who came with good references. In the end I sent out one hundred and nine applications, each one researched and personalised to the individual venue... and got four replies. One of those we couldn't make work, but we struck a deal with the remaining three and I began making arrangements for the trip.

Holland has always been a favourite destination of mine and it was a joy to be back there again, only this time presenting something of my own making. That trip went brilliantly well, and on top of playing music we had a lot of fun as we bonded further and worked our way across The Netherlands.

But changes in band personnel are almost inevitable, so I shouldn't have been surprised when things started to unravel. One of the more difficult things about being "the boss" is dealing with unrest in whatever form it takes. Our original bass player Ade had fallen foul of Rick, our lead guitarist. I hadn't been aware of any serious friction, but something had gone on and Rick refused to work with Ade any more. It was left to me to tell Ade the news, which wasn't pleasant and he was devastated, but I was left with no choice. The buck stopped with me.

In a chance conversation I found a top-class bass-playing replacement in Lyndon Webb. Another super feller and one of those multi-talented instrumentalists it's more than useful to have in any band.

Having got that situation settled, Marion decided her future chances lay elsewhere and she wanted out, too. I had built the band around Marion and her leaving was going to be the cause of many changes, but she felt she was following her own career path to greater glory. It didn't work out that way, as it so rarely does.

It was tough changing the set, finding and recruiting new personnel each time there was a vacancy. But setbacks are only temporary and demand a solution. I wasn't going to be beaten.

Graham was a guitarist and singer I'd seen playing in a pub. I knew he had a lot of something and deserved better than bashing out covers to a non-listening pub audience. We met up and over a drink discussed him coming on board. He was surprised to be asked but shouldn't have been. He was way good enough. Lots of rehearsals with new songs to learn, a raft of fine gigs, and a newly recorded EP ended when his partner ordered him to quit. It was a shame for Gray more than anyone. He's a lovely guy with a talent which will never be fulfilled with that weight to carry.

First Lyndon and, shortly after, Rick decided to go their own way. There was no fallout, just two people who had decided it was time to move on for their own reasons. For a short while I pondered on whether it was me. Was I such a bad boss? A tyrannical, demanding egotist? Someone who treated his bandmates with disdain and kept them on a meagre share of the "profits"? No, it was none of those things; far from it. This project had cost me thousands of pounds – buying a state-of-the-art van, putting everyone up in quality hotels, covering all the travelling costs, paying everybody a fee, and taking no money myself. It certainly wasn't a Dickensian regime. Perhaps, on reflection, I had made it too easy.

What was impossible to know in the revolving door of band members was that by chance we would end up with the best line-up The Jigantics has ever had. I'd like to think it was fate. On paper it shouldn't work so well, but in practice it does wonderfully.

I'd shared a stage with Sarah Kelly at a charity gig. She was playing ukulele wearing a colourful frock and delivering a mixture of her own songs and covers in an enchanting manner. Tall and incredibly slim, Sarah's beautiful vocals come with great stage presence and an ability to tell a story in song that is a rare gift. We didn't speak that day, but I was impressed. Sarah was another to be surprised when asked to join. What amazed me was that nobody had seen what was patently obvious and asked her before.

Back once more in Holland, an old friend of ours, Dick Barlage, requested Sarah sing a particular song he'd seen and heard her perform on YouTube. It was a song that reminded him of a girlfriend who had passed away. I said no as it didn't fit into our set, and although it would please one person, it had the potential to alienate everyone else. We had our set planned out for a reason and I was going to stick with it. As a compromise I suggested we do the song backstage during the interval, and everyone agreed. Dick, me, and our friend (the splendidly named Koen Hottentot) stood and listened as Sarah worked her way through the song. Dick was in floods of tears, and that deep emotion got to me as well. Afterwards I asked Sarah how she'd coped and got through it without faltering. Her reply was fascinating.

"I was aware that he was very upset," she said, "but I was in a different place at the time." It had never occurred to me that it was possible for anyone to be so inside a song but able to observe themselves from the outside. A kind of out-of-body experience. I still don't know how she does that.

Holding everything together in our Jigs quartet is guitarist Keith Thompson. Keith is a very fine English Blues/Rock guitarist who was more used to fronting his own band throughout the UK and Europe. Eastern Europe in particular is a place KT has toured successfully for decades. He answered a distress call from The Jigs and as a result became pivotal to everything the band do. Keith had no experience of the folk music scene and has adapted his playing style brilliantly to accommodate what the band needed.

His songwriting, lead and harmony vocals add another dimension to everything we do.

Mark Cole is a genius of sorts. Somehow, he gets a pleasing sound out of a variety of instruments, takes lead vocals, and fronts the band. I've known Mark for decades and he has never changed. He's always upbeat and the most even tempered, optimistic guy I've ever known. Laughter and all-round good humour are vital components when you're travelling and playing. Whatever the day throws at us, we get through partly due to Mark and his personality. He's irrepressible and irreplaceable.

Our quartet is really a quintet. Four of us are on stage, but Barb Granger is our agent, manager, driver, sound engineer, roadie, merchandiser, and more. The five of us are a team. She's been magnificent and turned us all into a musical family.

It seems likely that this band will see out my playing "career". Time catches up with us all and the future remains unknown. If that's how it pans out, I couldn't "leave the stage" with a better bunch of people than my buddies in this band. But until that time arrives, there's work to do and fun to be had.

# The Final Curtain

I knew when I started this book that I wasn't a writer. It didn't take me long to confirm that. Perhaps being an author is easier (although I have no intention of finding out) than writing a memoir. Fictional characters can be taken in any direction you want them to go. Speak any dialogue you care to invent on their behalf. Situations and plots, twists and turns can be manufactured from your imagination. In my case, I found it difficult trying to remember events and in particular dialogue of sixty-plus years ago with honesty and integrity. It was a challenge, but not a tortured one. I can't pretend that every word was torn from my soul with blood dripping onto the keyboard of my iPad or iPhone. The classic image of a writer alone in his garret save for a typewriter, a bottle of whisky, and a packet of cigarettes wasn't me. When I found a few minutes here and there, I jotted some words down wherever I happened to be. I did get days when I could sit and compose something in solitude, but that was in the comfort of home, a hotel lobby with time to kill, an airport lounge, or in one unusual but highly productive case, a dentist's waiting room.

Sometimes it flowed; most times it didn't. At times writing was interesting and at others emotional, reliving some of the more difficult moments. But I found myself grinning more often than grimacing in remembrance. I've been incredibly lucky in my life. Rudderless at times, drifting too often with the tide and not having a sense of direction, never mind an ultimate destination. However, overwhelmingly I have nothing to complain about. I've made mistakes, but hands up those who can say differently. I've said and done many stupid things that I still regret and can't undo, but I have been blessed in so many ways.

I've been asked why I decided to write a memoir at all. The honest answer is I don't know. It seemed a good idea at the time, which sums up much of my life. I was aware of some interest from those people who want to know every detail about the *Rocky Horror Show*. That was a motivation, I suppose, and the realisation that my story surrounding *Rocky* is unique, but only in the same way that we are all unique. The *Rocky Horror Show* doesn't define my life. It was a period of approximately two years. Had I concentrated solely on that, it would have made for a very short book.

One thing I did realise as I went through my life was how many of my friends are no longer with us. Kids I grew up with are no longer around. So many bandmates and friends who I spent thousands of hours with, are gone as well. Somewhere in my subconscious I must have decided if I was to tell my story, then now was the time to do so whilst I still could.

I hoped when I began writing that putting my life into some context would keep your interest. If you've managed to get this far, then I'm grateful. Thanks for sticking with it.

*Special thanks to Barbara Granger, Mark Cole and Tony Pazuzu, for all their help in making this project happen*